Praise for the new edition of
Winning the Loser's Game

"A must-*re*read classic, refreshed and updated with the latest 'lessons to be learned' from the 2008–2009 market events."
> —**Martin Leibowitz,** Managing Director,
> Morgan Stanley Research

"This is by far the best book on investment policy and management."
> —**Peter Drucker**

"No one understands what it takes to be a successful investor better than Charley Ellis and no one explains it more clearly or eloquently. This updated investment classic belongs on every investor's bookshelf."
> —**Consuelo Mack,** Anchor and Managing Editor,
> *Consuelo Mack WealthTrack*

"Charley Ellis has been one of the most influential investment writers for decades. This classic should be required reading for both individual and institutional investors."
> —**Burton Malkiel,** author,
> *A Random Walk Down Wall Street*

"Charley Ellis's classic—updated and even more accessible to everyone with an interest in investing and understanding markets—has long been required reading for professional investors. The latest edition is even more accessible to everyone with an interest in investing and under-standing markets. This elegant volume explores approaches for individuals such as relying on intellect, rather than emotion, and building a personal portfolio by taking advantage of what other investors already know. Ellis explores four key principals of successful long-term invest-ing and applies them to decisions by individuals, highlighting the importance of identifying your own goals and tolerance for portfolio risk and setting a suitable long-term course of action."
> —**Abby Joseph Cohen,** Goldman Sachs & Co.

"I am often asked by investors of all kinds, 'If you could read only one book about investing, what would it be?' The answer is simple: *Winning the Loser's Game*. Using compelling data and pithy stories, Charley Ellis has captured beautifully in this new and expanded edition of his classic work the most important lessons regarding investing. In today's unforgiving environment, it's a must read!"

—**F. William McNabb III,** Chief Executive Officer
and President, Vanguard

"Nowhere in this wise and prudent book will you learn to turn every $3 into $23 as Yale did in the 16 years Charley Ellis was on, and then chair of, its investment committee. Rather, you'll come to understand that in trying to beat the market your competition are players *like* Yale. Far better to beat 85% of the field merely by investing in index funds. That said, this is less a book about competition than about sound money management. Sounder than Charley Ellis they do not come."

—**Andrew Tobias,** author of *The Only
Investment Guide You'll Ever Need*

WINNING
THE LOSER'S
GAME

WINNING
THE LOSER'S
GAME

FIFTH EDITION

TIMELESS STRATEGIES for SUCCESSFUL INVESTING

CHARLES D. ELLIS

New York   Chicago   San Francisco   Lisbon   London
Madrid   Mexico City   Milan   New Delhi   San Juan
Seoul   Singapore   Sydney   Toronto

ISBN: 978-0-07-154549-5
MHID: 0-07-154549-2

This publication is designed to provide accurate and authoritative information in regard to the subject matter covered. It is sold with the understanding that neither the author nor the publisher is engaged in rendering legal, accounting, or other professional service. If legal advice or other expert assistance is required, the services of a competent professional person should be sought.

—From a Declaration of Principles jointly adopted
by a Committee of the American Bar Association
and a Committee of Publishers

McGraw-Hill books are available at special quantity discounts to use as premiums and sales promotions, or for use in corporate training programs. To contact a representative, please e-mail us at bulksales@mcgraw-hill.com.

CONTENTS

FOREWORD

In *Winning the Loser's Game*, Charley Ellis gets it right. As his classic evolved from the pithy *Investment Policy*, first published in 1985, to this more robust (but still concise) fifth edition, the central message remains—take charge of your portfolio and beware the blandishments of Wall Street.

Take-charge investors both understand and execute their own investment programs. When market participants follow this commonsense approach, investment results improve enormously. Self-reliant investors avoid many of Wall Street's counterproductive interventions that introduce conflicts of interest and reduce investment returns. Well-informed investors sidestep the wealth-diminishing actions of following the crowd and avoid entirely the schemes of charlatans like Bernie Madoff. Ever the wise coach, Charley counsels us to succeed by understanding ourselves and our investment alternatives.

Do It Yourself

Sensible investors rely on themselves. A strategy of professing ignorance and handing assets to a trained professional invites failure. How does an individual choose an investment advisor unless that individual understands enough to evaluate the prospective advisor's competence? Ironically, upon acquiring sufficient information to assess the skill of an investment service provider, individuals end up empowered to take control of their portfolios and make their own decisions.

Education begins with reading. Charley Ellis's *Winning the Loser's Game* represents a great starting point. Burt Malkiel's *A*

Random Walk Down Wall Street, Jack Bogle's *Bogle on Investing*, and my own *Unconventional Success* attempt to help individuals with the challenge of creating sensible investment programs. Each of these books outlines an easy-to-understand solution that could be distilled to two or three pages of prose. Why, then, do the books run hundreds of pages each? While it takes a short time to describe the conclusion, the bulk of the message provides the motivation for establishing a sensible program and the conviction for maintaining it through thick and thin. *Winning the Loser's Game* belongs at the top of the conviction-seeking reader's list.

The idea of taking charge of an investment portfolio daunts many investors. In fact, the correct solution involves pursuit of a basic, simple approach to markets that falls in the circle of competence of nearly everyone. As Charley so keenly observes, we need to "focus on what we cannot delegate—thinking for ourselves and acting for ourselves." After all, "That's how we make other decisions: whom to marry, where to live, whether to master a musical instrument, what sports to play, what ties to wear, and what to order in restaurants." Add managing your portfolio to your list of responsibilities.

A dearth of fiduciaries willing to place client interests foremost forces individuals to take responsibility for their investment portfolios. In the profit-motivated world of Wall Street, fiduciary responsibility takes a backseat to self-interest. What benefits the stockbroker (commissions), the mutual fund manager (large pools of assets), and the financial advisor (high fees) injures the investor. When profit motive meets fiduciary responsibility, profits win and investors lose.

Understand Your Investments

Two types of investors inhabit the investment world—a vanishingly small group that makes high-quality active management decisions and a much larger group that commands neither the resources nor the training to produce market-beating results. Membership in the active management cohort requires full-time dedication to understanding and exploiting market opportunities. Few qualify. Unfortunately, too many imagine that they possess active management skills, leading them to pursue costly strategies that all too predictably fail.

The overwhelmingly large number of investors should seek membership in the passive management club. This group, instead of scratching for a small edge in today's extraordinarily efficient markets, wisely accepts what the markets deliver. Charley makes a compelling case for the market-matching strategy of investing in index funds, touting their simplicity, transparency, low cost, tax efficiency, and superior returns.

Winning the Loser's Game contains a number of references to the chronic underperformance of mutual funds, for example, noting in Chapter 17 that over the past decade index funds beat the results of 80 percent of mutual funds. Shockingly, investors experience even worse results than those that Charley reports. First, the performance data necessarily exclude the results of the surprisingly large number of failed funds, a phenomenon known as "survivorship bias" (which Charley helpfully explains in Chapter 14). The pain for investors in failed mutual funds registers nowhere in an analysis of active funds. Second, the performance data do not account for taxes. Tax-efficient index funds garner a substantial edge over tax-inefficient actively managed mutual funds. Third, a distressingly large number of investors pay loads (front-end and deferred) to brokers when they purchase mutual funds. Because brokers impose these loads through a complex system of multiple share classes, they affect different classes of investors differently and do not appear in standard performance data. After adjusting the comparison of index funds to actively managed funds for survivorship bias, taxes, and loads, the dominance of index funds reaches insurmountable proportions.

Once investors recognize the primacy of index funds, the next step involves identifying an investment management firm. Wall Street, in its relentless quest for profits, manages to pervert even something as basic as a passive investment vehicle by charging excessive annual fees and imposing unjustifiable front-end or deferred loads. Fortunately, two major players operate on a not-for-profit basis, Vanguard and TIAA-CREF, both of which provide investors with high-quality products at rock-bottom prices. In fact, by shunning profits, Vanguard and TIAA-CREF eliminate the conflict between profit motive and fiduciary responsibility thus liberating the organizations to focus solely on serving investor interests. (*Note* that of the authors on my reading list, I serve on the board of TIAA, Jack Bogle founded Vanguard, and Burt Malkiel and Charley served on the board of Vanguard.)

In spite of Charley Ellis's compelling case for index funds, investor behavior falls far short of the ideal. Rational voices for sober investment practices achieve little notice in the cacophony of entertainment masquerading as advice (exemplified by MSNBC's Jim Cramer) and of advertisements promoting the hot fund of the month (propagated by the big for-profit mutual fund companies). As a result, at the end of 2007, index funds accounted for only slightly more than 5 percent of mutual fund assets, leaving almost 95 percent of assets in the hands of wealth-destroying active managers. In a rational world, the percentages would be reversed.

Charley admonishes investors to avoid the game of security selection and to focus on the business of asset allocation. Serious academic research supports his point. Roger Ibbotson, of Yale's School of Management, reports that more than 90 percent of the variability of investor returns comes from asset allocation, with security selection and market timing relegated to secondary and tertiary roles. Perhaps more important, asset allocation accounts for more than 100 percent of returns for the community of investors, as the negative-sum games of security selection and market timing detract from aggregate returns. Focus on asset allocation!

Understand Yourself

Risk tolerance plays a central role in the asset allocation decision. Successful investors fashion investment programs that address their unique circumstances and preferences. Even while recognizing that one-size-fits-all solutions fall short in the financial world, authors frequently proffer specific asset allocation suggestions or recommendations.

Charley Ellis, mindful of the limitations of broad-based advice, recommends portfolios dominated by equities. In fact, in Chapter 22 Ellis asserts that, "In your early years, you should definitely invest entirely in equities." Granted, he proposes a globally diversified portfolio of equities, while I prefer a more diversified approach with significant holdings of Treasury bonds and Treasury inflation-protected securities. Of course, matching each investor's risk tolerance with an appropriate portfolio ultimately matters most, not the generic portfolios proposed by Charley Ellis or me.

Self-understanding further contributes to investment success by helping investors avoid the all too human tendency to chase winners and to punish losers. Charley notes that investors too frequently buy high and sell low, both in selecting specific investments and in determining asset allocations.

A Sorry Tale

The story of a fund manager with a much celebrated 15-year streak of beating the S&P 500 illustrates the problems with active management and investor behavior. From the outset of his run on January 1, 1990, through its end on December 31, 2005, the hot-handed manager's return of 16.5 percent per annum easily beat the S&P 500's return of 11.5 percent per annum. So far, so good.

Unfortunately, all good things, including 15-year streaks, come to an end. From the beginning of 2006 to the end of 2008, the manager posted annual returns of −23.7 percent relative to −8.4 percent for the S&P 500. Fifteen fat years and three lean years produced an overall record of 8.6 percent per annum, measurably above the market return of 7.9 percent per annum.

Simple performance reports fail to capture the impact of these numbers on investor fortunes. At the inception of the extraordinary streak, funds under management amounted to only $800 million, exposing a relatively modest amount of investor assets to the beginning of the excitement. Fifteen years later, assets ballooned to $19.7 billion, placing the maximum level of investor funds at risk at the point of maximum bullishness. After three years of miserable performance and investor withdrawals, assets shrunk to a mere $4.3 billion.

Even though the simple time-weighted returns, as reported in fund offering documents and in fund advertisements, tell a story of modest market-beating results, dollar-weighted returns tell a different story. Taking into account investor cash flows, dollar-weighted returns fall short of the S&P 500 result by a margin of 7.0 percent per annum. Over the 18-year period that includes the 15-year streak and the 3-year fall from grace, the once-celebrated fund manager destroyed a staggering $3.6 billion of value for his investors.

The story of the first hot, then ice-cold fund manager exemplifies the pathology of the mutual fund industry. On the way up, the fund management company and the press lionize the manager, attracting attention to the winning strategy. Investors respond by throwing bushels of money at the seemingly invincible stock picker. Assets under management and performance peak simultaneously. Investors suffer as performance deteriorates. The fund management company, the press, and the public turn their attention elsewhere, ignoring the embarrassment of the fallen hero. The fund management company gets paid. The fund manager gets paid. The investor pays.

Charley Ellis

Charley Ellis sets the standard. In the late 1980s, several years after I took responsibility for managing Yale's endowment, I met Charley when he addressed a group of T. Rowe Price's investors at a meeting in Baltimore. Although I remember little else of that day—it was more than 20 years ago, after all—I vividly recall Charley telling us about the importance of his life-changing experiences at Phillips Exeter, Yale, and Harvard. As I heard him speak of his love for education, I knew I needed to know Charley.

In 1992, Charley joined Yale's investment committee. My colleagues and I eagerly anticipated his contributions to our meetings. We were never disappointed. Charley always advised gently, more often than not with superbly crafted stories (or Charley's parables, as we called them). Charley advanced Yale's interests in a manner that mattered immediately and resonated even more deeply as time passed. As just reward for his outstanding service, Charley took over the chair of Yale's investment committee in 1999.

When Charley joined the investment committee in 1992, Yale's fund stood just short of $3 billion. Sixteen years later, when he retired, Yale's assets totaled nearly $23 billion. To commemorate Charley's contributions to Yale's investment efforts, the investments office presented him with a calligraphic document, illuminated with Exeter silver, Yale blue, and Harvard crimson, thus closing the circle that began two decades earlier. Charley Ellis sets the standard.

David F. Swensen
Chief Investment Officer
Yale University
March 2009

PREFACE

If you are a 401(k) plan participant, chances are high that you want help deciding what to do and what *not* to do with your investments. That's why this short book was written for you.

Chances are also high that you are busy. That's why this book is short. And chances are high that you prefer candor and straight talk—particularly about money. Me too!

Lucky me! Married to a wonderful and inspiring woman, I was born in the United States; privileged in education; blessed with parents, children, and grandchildren I like, admire, and enjoy; and also blessed with an unusually wide circle of friends. I've had a fulfilling career in and around investment management—during a half century of growth and globalization.

Investment management is not only an endlessly fascinating profession, but it's also a most remarkably favored business replete with bright, engaged, and creative people. With all these advantages comes a clear responsibility to serve others. That's why I wrote this book.

With increasing concern, I've seen the long-term professionalism that attracted me to investing get increasingly compromised by short-term commercialism. My concern has been magnified by the accelerating shift from traditional "defined benefit" pension funds to "defined contribution" 401(k) plans. Most individuals don't know exactly what to do with their 401(k)s. They do know that an awful lot of "infomedia" is just advertising and is often misleading; they don't know where to turn to get the help they know they need. They are too busy to take the time to "learn all about it."

Retirement security plans have changed greatly. With pension plans, the plan sponsor takes responsibility for all the investing, and benefit payments come as long as we live. Not so with 401(k) plans where individuals are on their own for their most important investment decisions and where they run the risk of outliving their money and suffering the dreadful risk of poverty in their old age. While fine for some, self-directed "retirement security" is unhelpful for most—unless they get help on the basics and act wisely on a few central rules for success.

The securities markets have changed massively, creating an overwhelming problem for individual investors. That profound change is explained in Chapter 1, "The Loser's Game." Raised in a tradition that if you recognize a problem, you should look for a good solution, I've written this short book so that each reader can get to the place where he or she wants to be on questions of financial security: understanding the realities he or she faces and knowing how to take appropriate action and convert a loser's game into a winner's game in which every sensible investor can and will be a long-term winner.

As Winston Churchill so wisely observed, "People like winning very much!" We all like winning with investments, and we all can win—at lower cost, less risk, and less time and effort by knowing our real objectives, developing a sensible strategy, and sticking with it for the long term so that the markets are working for us.

William S. Rukeyser, the extraordinary editor and cheerful language disciplinarian, took the time and care to simplify, clarify, and strengthen every part of this book from selecting specific words to reordering paragraphs and removing redundancies. He made it easier and better for every reader.[1] Bill helped me get close to my grandmother's high hope as I left home for college that I would not only read a lot of writing, but I would also learn how to write reading.

Shaken by stunning losses in the recent terrible markets—driven by an awful global economic crisis—investors are sensibly asking: What's different now? How have the investment principles changed? The core principles of successful investing *never* change—and never will. In fact, when short-term data appear to be most challenging to core principles is exactly when those principles are most important and most needed. Sure the companies, markets, and economies come and go, but the core principles remain the same. That's why, when you've read this book, you'll know all you really need to know to be successful in investing your 401(k).

End Note

1 If Bill's editing saves every reader one hour and another 100,000 people read this book, Bill will have saved the equivalent of 50 *years* of work. Not bad for a month's effort!

CHAPTER 1

THE LOSER'S GAME

DISAGREEABLE DATA ARE STREAMING STEADILY OUT OF THE computers of performance measurement firms. Over and over again these facts and figures inform us that mutual funds are failing to "perform" or beat the market. Occasional periods of above-average results raise expectations that are soon dashed as false hopes. Contrary to their often-articulated goal of outperforming the market averages, the nation's investment managers are not beating the market; the market is beating them.

Faced with information that contradicts what they believe, people tend to respond in one of two ways. Some ignore the new knowledge and hold to their former beliefs. Others accept the validity of the new information, factor it into their perception of reality, and put it to use. Most investment managers and most individual investors, being in a sustained state of denial, are holding onto a set of romantic beliefs developed in a long-gone era of different markets. Their romantic views of "investment opportunity" are repeatedly proving to be costly.

Investment management, as traditionally practiced, is based on a single basic belief: Investors *can* beat the market. Times have changed the markets, and that premise now appears to be false even for most professional investment managers. (See Figures 1.1 and 1.2.)

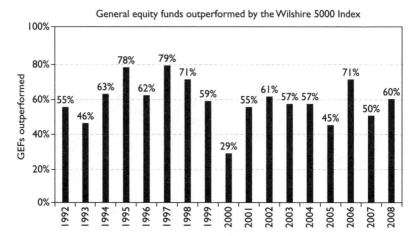

Figure 1.1 Total market versus Wilshire 5000 Index
As shown above, in most years a majority of equity funds are beaten by the market. It gets worse during large periods of time, such as over a decade, where 68 percent of equity funds get beaten by the market.

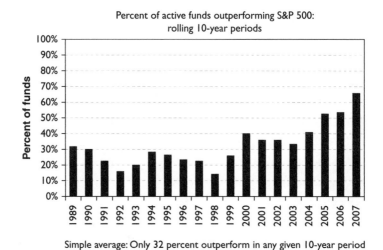

Simple average: Only 32 percent outperform in any given 10-year period

Figure 1.2 Only 32 percent of equity mutual funds outperform the S&P 500, 1989–2008

If the premise that it is feasible to outperform the market were true, then deciding *how* to go about achieving success would be a matter of straightforward logic.

First, since the overall market can be represented by a public listing such as the Wilshire 5000 Total Market Index, a successful manager would only need to rearrange his or her portfolios more productively than the "mindless" index. The manager could be different in stock selection, strategic emphasis on particular groups of stocks, market timing, or various combinations of these strategies.

Second, since an active manager would want to make as many "right" decisions as possible, he or she would assemble a group of bright, well-educated, highly motivated, hardworking professionals whose collective purpose would be to identify underpriced securities to buy and overpriced securities to sell—and beat the market by shrewdly betting against the crowd.

Unhappily, the basic assumption that most institutional investors can outperform the market is false. The institutions *are* the market. They cannot, as a group, outperform themselves. In fact, given the cost of active management—fees, commissions, market impact of big transactions, and so forth—85 percent of investment managers have and will continue over the long term to underperform the overall market.

Because investing institutions are so numerous and capable and determined to do well for their clients, professional investment management is not a "winner's game." That's why a large majority of mutual funds, pension funds, and endowments are not successful: Professional investing has become a *loser's* game.

Individual investors investing on their own do even worse—on average, much worse. (Day trading is the worst of all: A sucker's game. Don't do it—ever.)

Before analyzing what happened to convert institutional investing from a winner's game to a loser's game, consider the profound difference between these two kinds of games. In a winner's game, the outcome is determined by the correct actions of the *winner*. In a loser's game, the outcome is determined by mistakes made by the *loser*.

Dr. Simon Ramo, a scientist and one of the founders of TRW Inc., identified the crucial difference between a winner's game and a loser's game in an excellent book on game strategy, *Extraordinary Tennis for the Ordinary Tennis Player*.[1] Over many years Dr. Ramo observed that tennis is not one game but two: one played by professionals and a very few gifted amateurs, the other played by all the rest of us.

Although players in both games use the same equipment, dress, rules, and scoring, and both conform to the same etiquette and customs, they play two very different games. After extensive statistical analysis, Ramo summed it up this way: Professionals *win* points; amateurs *lose* points.

In expert tennis the ultimate outcome is determined by the actions of the *winner*. Professional tennis players stroke the ball hard with laserlike precision through long and often exciting rallies until one player is able to drive the ball just out of reach or force the other player to make an error. These splendid players seldom make mistakes.

Amateur tennis, Ramo found, is almost entirely different. The outcome is determined by the loser. Here's how. Brilliant shots, long and exciting rallies, and seemingly miraculous recoveries are few and far between. The ball is all too often hit into the net or out of bounds, and double faults at service are not uncommon. Instead of trying to add power to our serve or hit closer to the line to win, we should concentrate on consistently getting the ball back. Amateurs seldom beat their opponents but instead beat themselves. The victor in this game of tennis gets a higher score *because the opponent is losing even more points.*

As a scientist and statistician, Ramo gathered data to test his hypothesis in a clever way. Instead of keeping conventional game scores—15 love, 15 all, 30–15, and so forth—Ramo simply counted points *won* versus points *lost*. He found that in expert tennis about 80 percent of the points are *won*, whereas in amateur tennis about 80 percent of the points are *lost*.

The two games are fundamental opposites. Professional tennis is a winner's game: The outcome is determined by the actions of the winner. Amateur tennis is a loser's game: The outcome is determined by the actions of the loser, who defeats himself or herself.

The distinguished military historian Admiral Samuel Eliot Morison makes a similar central point in his thoughtful treatise *Strategy and Compromise*: "In warfare, mistakes are inevitable. Military decisions are based on estimates of the enemy's strengths and intentions that are usually faulty, and on intelligence that is never complete and often misleading. Other things being equal," concludes Morison, "the side that makes the fewest strategic errors wins the war."[2]

War is the ultimate loser's game. Amateur golf is another. Tommy Armour, in his book *How to Play Your Best Golf All the Time*[3], says: "The best way to win is by making fewer bad shots." This is an observation with which all weekend golfers would concur.

There are many other loser's games. Like institutional investing, some were once winner's games but have changed into loser's games with the passage of time. For example, 90 years ago only very brave, athletic, strong-willed young people with good eyesight had the nerve to try flying an airplane. In those glorious days, flying was a winner's game. But times have changed, and so has flying. If the pilot of your 747 came aboard today wearing a 50-mission hat and a long white silk scarf around his or her neck, you'd get off. Such people no longer belong in airplanes because flying today is a loser's game with one simple rule: Don't make any mistakes.

Often, winner's games self-destruct because they attract too many players, all of whom want to win. (That's why gold rushes finish ugly.) The "money game" we call investment management evolved in recent decades from a winner's game to a loser's game because a basic change has occurred in the investment environment: The market came to be dominated in the 1970s and 1980s by the very institutions that were striving to win by outperforming the market. No longer is the active investment manager competing with cautious custodians or amateurs who are out of touch with the market. Now he or she competes with other hardworking investment experts in a loser's game where the secret to winning is to lose less than the others lose.

Today's money game includes a formidable group of competitors. Several thousand institutional investors—hedge funds, mutual funds, pension funds, and others—operate in the market all day, every day, in the most intensely competitive way. Among the 50 largest and most active institutions, even the smallest spends $100 million in a typical year buying services from the leading broker-dealers in New York, London, Frankfurt, Tokyo, Hong Kong, and Singapore. Understandably, these formidable competitors always get the "first call" with important new information. Thus, about half the time that we individual investors buy and about half the time we sell, the "other fellow" is one of those giant professionals, with all their experience and all their information and all their analytical resources.

The key question under the new rules of the game is this: How much better must the active mutual fund investment manager be to at least recover the costs of active management? The answer is daunting. If we assume 100 percent portfolio turnover (implying that the fund manager holds a typical stock for 12 months, which is slightly longer than average for the mutual fund industry) and we assume total trading costs (commissions plus the impact of big trades on market prices) of 1 percent to buy and 1 percent to sell (again, average rates), plus 1.25 percent in fees and expenses for active management, the typical fund's operating costs are

3.25 percent per year.[4] (A few well-managed mutual funds, such as the American Funds, are longer-term investors and therefore have much lower turnover, lower operating costs, and better results.)

Recovering these costs is surprisingly difficult in a market dominated by professional investors who are intensely competitive, extraordinarily well informed, and continuously active—and who make few large operational *micro*-mistakes. (Even the pros make *macro*-mistakes, particularly being fully invested together at market peaks, or choosing dot com stocks together.) When they do make micro-mistakes, they correct their errors quickly or see them exploited and quickly "corrected" by their professional competitors. (Individual investors make more macro-mistakes—going with the crowd when "everyone knows" it's a new dot-com era or fears a global credit collapse.) An active manager must overcome the drag of 3.25 percent on annual operating costs. If the fund manager is only to match the market's historical 10 percent return after all costs, he or she must return 13.25 percent before all those costs. In other words, for you merely to do as well as the market, your fund manager must be able to outperform the market return by—nearly one-third—32.5 percent![5]

That's why the stark reality is that most money managers and their clients *have not* been winning the money game. They have been losing. The historical record shows that on a cumulative basis, over three-quarters of professionally managed mutual funds *under*perform the S&P 500 stock market index. And for active individual investors, the record is even worse. Thus the burden of proof is on the person who says, "I am a winner; I will win the money game."

For any one manager to outperform the other professionals, he or she must be so skillful and so quick that he or she can regularly catch the other professionals making mistakes—and systematically exploit those mistakes faster than the other professionals.

(The alternative approach—"slow investing"—is to base decisions on research with a long-term focus that will catch other investors obsessing about the short term and cavitating—producing bubbles.)

Working *efficiently*, as Peter Drucker so wisely explained, means knowing how to do things the right way, but working *effectively* means doing the right things. Since most investment managers will not beat the market, investors should at least consider investing in "index funds" that replicate the market and so *never* get beaten by the market. Indexing may not be fun or exciting, but it works. The data from the performance measurement firms show that index funds have outperformed most investment managers over long periods of time.

The reason investing has become a loser's game for the professionals who manage most of the leading mutual funds and investment management organizations is that their efforts to beat the market are no longer the most important part of the solution; they are now the most important part of the problem. As we learn in game theory, each player's strategy should incorporate understanding and anticipation of the strategies and behavior of other players. In the complex problem each investment manager is trying to solve, his or her efforts to find a solution—and the efforts of the many determined competitors—have become the dominant adverse variables facing active managers.

For most investors, the hardest part is not figuring out the optimal investment policy; it is staying committed to sound investment policy through bull and bear markets and maintaining what Disraeli called "constancy to purpose." Sustaining a long-term focus at market highs or market lows is notoriously difficult. At either market extreme, emotions are strongest when current market action appears most demanding of change and the apparent "facts" seem most compelling.

Being rational in an emotional environment is never easy. Holding onto a sound policy through thick and thin is both extraordinarily difficult *and* extraordinarily important work. This is why investors can benefit from developing and sticking with sound investment policies and practices. The cost of infidelity to your own commitments can be very high.

An investment counselor's proper professional priority is to help each client identify, understand, and commit consistently and continually to long-term investment objectives that are both realistic in the capital markets and appropriate to that particular investor's true objectives. Investment counseling helps investors choose the right objectives.

It's not active managers' fault that their results are so disappointing. The competitive environment within which they work has changed dramatically in 50 years from quite favorable to very adverse—and it is getting worse and worse.

Before examining the changes in the investment climate, let's remind ourselves that active investing is, at the margin, *always* a negative-sum game. Trading investments among investors would by itself be a zero-sum game, except that costs such as commissions, expenses, and market impact must be deducted. These costs total in the hundreds of billions every year. Net result: Active investing is a seriously negative-sum game.

To achieve better than average results through active management, you depend directly on exploiting the mistakes and blunders of others. Others must be acting as though they are *willing to lose* so that you can win after covering all your costs of operation. Even in the 1960s, when institutions did only 10 percent of the public trading and individual investors did 90 percent, large numbers of amateurs were realistically bound to lose to the professionals. We can understand why this was—and is—the reality of the situation by reviewing some of the characteristics of individual investors.

Individual investors usually buy for reasons *outside* the stock market: They buy because they inherit money, get a bonus, sell a house, or, for any other happy reason, have money to invest as a result of something that has no direct connection to the stock market. Similarly, they sell stocks because a child is going off to college or they have decided to buy a home—almost always for reasons *outside* the stock market. Candidly, when individuals act because of reasons they think are *inside* the market, they are usually making a mistake; they are either optimistic and late because the market has been rising or pessimistic and late during a falling market.

In addition, compared to the full-time well-organized institutions, individual investors typically do not do extensive, rigorous comparison-shopping across the many alternatives within the stock market. Most individual investors are not experts on even a few companies. Many rely for information from newspapers, cable television, the Internet, friends, or retail stockbrokers—many of whom are seldom experts. Individuals may *think* they know something important when they invest, but almost always what they think they know is either not true or not relevant or not important new information. The amateur's "scoop" is already known and factored into the market price by the professionals who are active in the market all the time. Thus, the activity of most individual investors is what market researchers correctly call "informationless" trading or "noise." (These terms are not rude; they are simply descriptive. Anyone who feels offended by them is just being too sensitive.)

It is little wonder that back in the 1950s and 1960s professional investors—who were always working *inside* the market, making rigorous and well-informed comparisons of price to value across hundreds and hundreds of different stocks on which they could command up-to-the-minute information—thought they could outperform the individual investors who dominated the stock market and did 90 percent of all the trading. Back then, the professionals could and did outperform the amateurs. But that was half a century ago.

The picture is profoundly different now. After 50 years of enormous growth in mutual funds, pension funds, and hedge funds *and* increasing turnover in those institutions' portfolios, the old 90:10 ratio has been completely reversed. Today 90 percent of all New York Stock Exchange (NYSE) "public" trades are made by investment professionals. In fact, 75 percent of all trading is done by the professionals at the 100 largest and most active institutions, and fully half of all NYSE trading is done by the professionals at just the 50 largest and most active institutional investors.

Just how good and tough to beat are the hundred largest institutions? Here are some realities: The very largest institutions each pay Wall Street $1 billion annually and pay their leading stockbrokers as much as $100 million *apiece*, and the stockbrokers earn it by making the best markets and providing the best research services they can deliver. The institutions have Bloomberg and all the other sophisticated information services. Their professionals meet with corporate management frequently. They all have teams of in-house analysts and senior portfolio managers with an average of 20 years of investing experience—all working their contacts and networks to get the best information all the time. You get the picture: Compared to any individual investor, the institution has all the advantages.

And what tough professionals they are! Top of their class in college and at graduate school, they are "the best and the brightest"—disciplined and rational, supplied with extraordinary information by thousands of analysts who are highly motivated, hardworking, and very competitive—and all are playing to *win*. Sure, professionals make errors and mistakes, but the other pros are always looking for any error and will pounce on it. Important new investment opportunities simply don't come along all that often, and the few that do certainly don't stay undiscovered for long. Yes, several mutual funds beat the market in any particular year and some in any decade, but scrutiny of the long-term records reveals that only a few mutual funds beat the market averages over the long haul— and nobody has yet figured out how to tell in advance which funds will do it.

"Regression to the mean" (the tendency for behavior to move toward "normal" or average) is a persistently powerful phenomenon in physics and sociology—and in investing. Thus, as a group, professional investment managers are so good that they make it nearly impossible for any one professional to outperform the market they together now dominate.

Even more discouraging to investors searching for superior managers is that those managers who have had superior results in the *past* are not likely to have superior results in the *future.* In investment performance, the past is *not* prologue except for the grim finding that those who have repetitively done particularly badly are unlikely to break out of their slough of despair and do well.

The encouraging truth is that while most investors are doomed to lose if they play the loser's game of trying to beat the market, every investor can be a long-term winner. All we need to do to be long-term winners is to reorient ourselves to concentrate on realistic long-term goal setting and staying the course with sensible investment policies that will achieve our own particular objectives by applying the self-discipline, patience, and fortitude required for persistent implementation. That's what this book is all about: redefining the objective of the "game" and playing the true winner's game.

End Notes

1. Simon Ramo, *Extraordinary Tennis for the Ordinary Tennis Player* (New York: Crown Publishers, 1977).
2. Samuel Eliot Morison, *Strategy and Compromise* (New York: Little Brown, 1958).
3. Tommy Armour, *How to Play Your Best Golf All the Time* (New York: Simon & Schuster, 1971).
4. More than brokerage commissions and dealer spreads are properly included in transaction costs. The best way to show how high transactions costs are is to compare the theoretical results of a "paper portfolio" with the actual results of a "real money portfolio." Experts will tell you that the differences are impressive. And there's yet another cost of transactions—the cost of unwisely getting into stocks you would not have purchased if you were not "sure" you could get out at any time because the market looked so liquid. This is a real liquidity trap. Think how differently people would behave on the highway or in the bedroom if they were sure they would be caught. It's the same way in investments: You don't always get caught, nor do you always not get caught. All these costs are part of the total transactions costs.
5. This makes the superior performance of Warren Buffett of Berkshire Hathaway and David Swensen of Yale all the more wonderful to behold.

CHAPTER 2

BEATING THE MARKET

THE ONLY WAY ACTIVE INVESTMENT MANAGERS CAN BEAT THE market, after adjusting for market risk, is to discover and exploit other investors' mistakes.

It can be done, and it has been done by many investors *some* of the time. However, very few investors have been able to outsmart and outmaneuver other investors often enough and regularly enough to beat the market consistently over the long term, particularly after covering all the costs, including the taxes, of "playing the game."

In theory, active investment managers can try to succeed with any or all of four investment approaches:

- Market timing.
- Selecting specific stocks or groups of stocks.
- Making timely changes in portfolio structure or strategy.
- Developing and implementing a superior, long-term investment concept or philosophy.

Even the most casual observer of markets and companies will be impressed by the splendid array of apparent—and enticing—opportunities to do better than "settle for average." The major changes in price charts for the overall market, for major industry groups, and for individual stocks make it seem deceptively "obvious" that active investors *must* be able to do better. After all, we've seen with our own eyes that the real stars perform consistently better than average in such diverse fields as sports, theater, and medicine, so why not in investing? Why shouldn't quite a few investment managers be consistently above average? In short, why should it be all that hard to beat the market?

The most audacious way to increase potential returns is through "market timing." The classic "market timer" moves the portfolio in and out of the market so that it is, he or she hopes, fully invested during rising markets and substantially out of the market when prices are falling badly. Another form of timing would shift an equity portfolio out of stock groups that are expected to underperform the market and into groups expected to outperform.

But remember: Every time you decide to get out of the market *or* get in, the investors you buy from or sell to are professionals. Of course, the pros are not *always* right, but how confident are you that you will be "more right" more often than they will be? What's more, market timers incur trading costs with each and every move. And unless you are managing a tax-sheltered retirement account, you will have to pay taxes every time you take a profit. Over and over, the "benefits" of market timing prove illusory. The costs are real—and keep adding up.

Investment history documents conclusively that the very first weeks of a market recovery produce a substantial proportion of all the gains that will eventually be experienced. Yet it is at the crucial market bottom that a market timer is most likely to be out of the market—missing the very best part of the gains.

In a bond portfolio, the market timer hopes to shift into long maturities before falling interest rates drive up long-bond prices and back into short maturities before rising interest rates drive down long-bond prices. In a balanced portfolio, the market timer strives to invest more heavily in stocks when they will produce greater total returns than bonds, then shift into bonds when they will produce greater total returns than stocks, and then into short-term investments when they will produce greater total returns than either bonds or stocks. Unfortunately, on average, these moves just don't work. And the more often any are tried, the more certainly they fail to work.

Market timing does not work because no manager is much more astute or insightful—on a repetitive basis—than his or her professional competitors. In addition, much of the stock market "action" occurs, as we shall see, in very brief periods and at times when investors are most likely to be captives of a conventional consensus.

Perhaps the best insight into the difficulties of market timing came from an experienced professional's candid lament: "I've seen lots of interesting approaches to market timing—and I have tried most of them in my 40 years of investing. They may have been great before my time, but not one of them worked for me. Not one!"

Just as there are *old* pilots and *bold* pilots, but no old, bold pilots, there are almost *no* investors who have achieved recurring successes in market timing. Decisions that are driven by greed or fear are usually wrong, usually late, and unlikely to be reversed correctly. The market does just as well, on average, when the investor is *out* of the market as it does when he or she is *in* it. Therefore, the investor loses money relative to a simple buy-and-hold strategy by being out of the market part of the time. Wise investors don't even *consider* trying to outguess the market or out-maneuver the professionals by selling high and buying low.

One reason is particularly striking. Figure 2.1 shows what happens to long-term compounded returns when the best days are removed from the record. Taking out the 10 best days—less than one-quarter of 1 percent of the long period examined—cuts the average rate of return by 17 percent (from 18 percent to 15 percent). Taking the 10 next best days away cuts returns

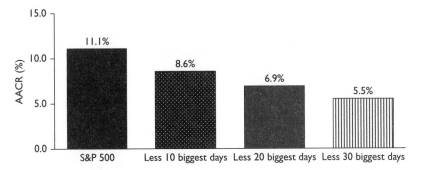

Source: Courtesy of Cambridge Associates

Figure 2.1 Compound returns (%), 1980–2008

by another 3 percent. Removing a total of 30 days—just half of 1 percent of the total period—cuts returns almost by 40 percent, from 18 percent to 11 percent. Figure 2.2 shows a similar result when the best *years* are excluded from the calculation of the long-term averages.

Using the S&P 500 average returns, the story is told quickly and clearly: *All* the total returns on stocks in the past 75 years were achieved in the best 60 *months*—less than 7 percent of the 800 months of those long decades. (Imagine the profits if we could simply know which months! Alas, we cannot and never will.)

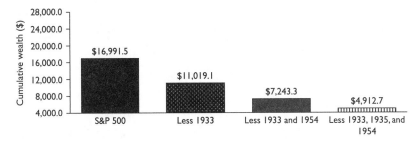

Source: Courtesy of Cambridge Associates

Figure 2.2 Cumulative returns on $1 invested, 1928–2000

What we do know is both simple and valuable: If you missed those few and fabulous 60 best months, you would have missed all the total returns accumulated over three full generations.

A $1 investment in the S&P 500 that missed the 90 best trading days in a recent 10-year period would have *lost* money (22 cents) and would have made only 30 cents if it missed the best 60 days—but would have made $5.59 by staying fully invested. (Seductively, for those willing to be seduced, sidestepping the 90 *worst* trading days would have resulted in a 10-year gain of $42.78.) Removing just the five best *days* out of 72 *years* of investing would reduce cumulative compound returns—without dividend investments—by nearly 50 percent.[1]

One of the ways investors hurt themselves over the long run is to get frightened out of the market when the market has been awful. They miss the surprisingly important best days. If, for example, an investor missed just the 10 best days over the past 109 years he or she would miss two-thirds of the total gains—that's 10 days out of 39,812 days—reports Jason Zweig.[2]

That's why most active investors tempted by market timing should carefully consider Mies van der Rohe's admonition on architecture: "Less is more." The lesson is clear: You have to be there "when lightning strikes." That's why market timing is a truly wicked idea. Don't try it—ever.

The second tactical way to increase returns is through "stock selection," or "stock picking." Professional investors devote extraordinary skill, time, and effort to this work. Stock valuation dominates the research efforts of investing institutions and the research services of stockbrokers all over the world.

Through financial analysis and field research on competitors and suppliers as well as management interviews, professional investors strive to attain an understanding of the investment value of a security or a group of securities that is better than the market consensus. When investment managers find significant differences between the market price and the value of a security as they appraise it, they can buy or sell, trying to capture for their clients' portfolios the differential between the market's price and the true investment value.

Unfortunately, however, security analysis taken as a whole does not appear to be a profitable activity. The stocks investment managers sell after doing fundamental research and the stocks they don't buy typically do about as well as the stocks they do buy. As they sell to one another and buy from one another, academics say they are making the market pricing mechanism "efficient."

The problem is not that investment research is not done well. The problem is that research is done very well by many. Research analysts at major brokerage firms share their information and evaluations almost instantly through global information networks with thousands of professional investors who take swift action, often striving to act quickly in anticipation of how others will soon act. As a result, no single group of investors is likely to gain and sustain a repetitive useful advantage over all other investors on stock selection. Because they are so large, so well-informed, and so active, institutional investors set the prices. That's why the only way to beat the market is to beat the professionals who, as a group, *are* the market.

Strategic decisions in both stock and bond portfolios involve major commitments that affect the overall structure of the portfolio. They are the third way to try to increase returns. They are made to exploit insights into major industry groups, changes in the economy and interest rates, or anticipated shifts in the valuation of major types of stocks, such as "emerging growth" stocks or "value" stocks. Each of these judgments involves what can best be described as market-segment risk. As the well-worn saying goes, it is not a stock market but a "market of stocks"—one that lures investors into painful market traps.

Full of interesting potential—being in the right place at the right time—this approach to investing challenges the investor to discover a new (and often unfamiliar) way to invest as markets shift, to become proficient at each new way, and then to abandon that new way for another new way. In theory, of course, this can be done, but *will* it be done? Sure, it will be done occasionally, but by which managers? And for how long? The long-term record is not encouraging. And the record of individual investors identifying—in advance—which managers will succeed is downright discouraging.

For example, in the late 1990s, those investors who were most committed to technology enjoyed a wonderful romp—until the sharp market "correction" in 2000. The market giveth, and the market taketh away. Then, in the early part of the first decade of the twenty-first century, financial stocks did well—until they led to the 2008–2009 market collapse.

In the early 1970s, portfolio managers who invested heavily in large-capitalization growth stocks—the "Nifty 50"—experienced exceptionally favorable results as the notorious "two tier" market continued to develop. (Growth stocks had a much higher P/E—price/earnings—ratio than industrial stocks, dividing the market into two tiers.) But by the later 1970s, owning the same securities produced exceptionally negative results: Anticipated earnings failed to materialize, and investors became disenchanted with the whole "hold forever" concept and dumped their holdings. The same thing happened with oil stocks in the eighties, major pharmaceuticals in the nineties, and commodities in the first decade of the twenty-first century. All too often, at the peak, the confident consensus is, "This time it's different!" The same up, up, up, *down* phenomenon has been repeated many times.

Another possible way to increase returns is for an individual portfolio manager or an entire investment management organization to develop a profound and valid insight into the forces that will drive superior long-term investment results in a particular sector of the market or a particular group of companies or industries and to systematically exploit that investment insight or concept through cycle after cycle in the stock market and in the business economy.

An investment fund organization that is committed, for example, to growth-stock investing will concentrate on evaluating new technologies, understanding the management skills required to lead rapidly growing organizations, and analyzing the financial requirements for investing in new markets and new products to sustain growth. This organization will strive to learn from experience—sometimes painful experience—how to discriminate between ersatz growth stocks that fizzle out and true growth companies that will achieve serial successes over many years.

Other fund managers take the view that, among the many large corporations in mature and often cyclical industries, there are always some that have considerably greater investment value than most investors recognize. With astute research, these managers believe that they can isolate superior values and, by buying good value at depressed prices, achieve superior returns for their clients with relatively low risk. Such organizations strive to develop expertise in separating the wheat from the chaff, avoiding the low-priced stocks that really *ought* to be low priced.

The important test of an investment concept or philosophy is the manager's ability to adhere to it persistently for valid, long-term reasons even when the short-term results are disagreeable. Persistence can lead to distinctive competence in the particular kind of investing in which a manager specializes.

The great advantage of the conceptual or philosophical approach is that the investment firm can organize itself to do its own particular kind of investing all the time, avoid the noise and confusion of distracting alternatives, attract investment analysts and managers interested in and skilled at the particular type of investing, and, through continuous practice, self-critique, and study, develop real mastery. The great disadvantage is that if the chosen kind of investing becomes obsolete, overpriced, or out of touch with the changing market, a focused, specialist organization is unlikely to detect the need for change until it becomes too late—for its clients and for itself.

What is remarkable about profound investment concepts is how few have been discovered that have lasted for long—most likely because the hallmark of a free capital market is that few if any opportunities to establish a proprietary long-term competitive conceptual advantage can be found and maintained for a long time. The markets for good ideas are among the best in the world: Word gets around very quickly.

All of these basic forms of active investing have one fundamental characteristic in common: *They depend on the errors of others.* Whether by omission or commission, the only way a profit opportunity can be available to an active investor is for the consensus of other professional investors to be *wrong*. While this sort of collective error does occur, we must ask how often these errors are made and how often any particular manager will avoid making the same errors and instead have the wisdom, skill, and courage to take action opposed to the consensus.

With so many competitors simultaneously seeking superior insight into the value/price relationship of individual stocks or industry groups and with so much information so widely and rapidly communicated throughout the investment community, the chances of discovering and exploiting profitable insights into individual stocks or groups of stocks—opportunities left behind by the errors and inattention of other investors—are certainly not richly promising.

However, there are other kinds of opportunities for achieving more success as a long-term investor. One way to increase success in lifelong investing is to reduce mistakes and errors. Ask any golfer or tennis player how beneficial reducing errors can be.

One mistake many investors make is "trying too hard"—striving to get more from their investments than those investments can produce. Trying too hard—and thus courting disappointment—is all too often eventually expensive because taking too much risk *is* too much risk.

An opposite mistake investors all too often make is "not trying hard enough"—usually by being cautious only for short-term reasons when successful investing requires long-term thinking and long-term behavior. Being too defensive—letting short-term anxieties dominate long-term thinking and acting—can be expensive. While 2008 was clearly a dramatic exception, over the long term it has been costly to hold even a modest cash "reserve" within an equity portfolio or to concentrate bond investments in U.S. governments.

With so many apparent "opportunities" to do better than the market, it must be difficult and disconcerting for investors to accept how hard it is to do better than the market over the long haul. Even the most talented investment manager must wonder how he or she can expect his or her hardworking and determined competitors to provide him or her—through incompetence, error, or inattention—with sufficiently attractive opportunities to buy or sell on significantly advantageous terms on such a regular basis that he or she can beat the market by beating them.

In the movie *Full Metal Jacket*, two crusty drill sergeants are watching their basic training class jogging in close-order drill to their graduation ceremony, shouting military calls like "Airborne! All the way!" One drill instructor says, "Sarge, what do you see when you look at those boys?" After the classic expectoration, the other replies, "What do I see? I'll tell ya. About 10 percent of those boys are honest to God *soldiers!*" Pause. "The rest . . . are just . . . targets!" That's just a scene from a war flick, but it may have real-life meaning for you as an investor to ponder.

Here's a way to turn on the lights. Let's assume that you are so skilled and so well informed that you are in fact in the top 20 percent of all individual investors. Bravo! Take a bow—but watch out! Here's why. Even if you are a far *above*-average investor, you are almost certain to be making *below*-average trades or investment decisions. It's in the numbers.

The first step into reality is to recognize that the key to market success is *not* the skill and knowledge of the *investor* compared to other individual investors, but the skill and knowledge with which *each* specific investment *transaction* is made.

The second step is to recognize and accept the reality that 75 percent of all the trades on the NYSE are made by the 100 largest and most active institutional investors, and it's just possible that almost all of them trade better than you do and highly likely that three-quarters of them trade better. Even if you were among the very best amateurs, that would make your transactions *below* average. And if 90 percent of the pros trade with more skill than you have—which is, alas, almost certain—your transactions will, on average, be deep in the bottom quartile.

In a paper titled "Why *Do* Investors Trade Too Much?" Terrance Odean, finance professor at the University of California at Berkeley looked at nearly 100,000 stock trades made by retail investors at a major discount brokerage firm from 1987 through 1993. He found that on average the stocks these investors bought underperformed the market by 2.7 percentage points over the following year, while the stocks they sold outperformed the market by 0.5 point in the following year. Similarly, a paper published by Brookings Institution economists Josef Lakonishok, Andrei Shleifer, and Robert Vishny showed that the stock trades made by professional fund managers subtracted 0.78 percent from the returns they would have earned by keeping their portfolios constant. Finally, the Plexus Consulting Group, a firm that researches the costs of trading for professional money managers, studied more than 80,000 trades by 19 investment firms and found that the typical purchase of a stock added 0.67 percent to a fund's short-term return but that the typical sale subtracted 1.08 percent. No wonder Philip Carret, the founder of the Pioneer Fund, said, "Turnover usually indicates a failure of judgment. It's extremely difficult to figure out when to sell anything."

Las Vegas, Macao, and Monaco are busy every day, so we know not everyone is rational. If you, like Walter Mitty, still fantasize that you can and will beat the pros, you'll need both good luck and our prayers.

This inevitably raises the central question: If you can't beat the 100 largest and most active institutions, why not join them?

Experienced investors all understand four wonderfully powerful truths about investing, and wise investors govern their investing by adhering to these four great truths:

1. The dominating reality is that the most important investment decision is your long-term mix of assets: how much in stocks, real estate, bonds, or cash.
2. That mix should be determined partly by the real purpose—growth, income, safety, and so on—and mostly according to when the money will be used.
3. Diversify within each asset class and between asset classes. Bad things do happen—usually as surprises.
4. Be patient and persistent. Good things come in spurts—usually when least expected—and fidgety investors fare badly. "Plan your play and play your plan," say the great coaches. "Stay the course" is usually wise. So is setting the right course—which takes you back to #1.

Curiously, most active investors—who all say they are trying to get "better performance"—do themselves and their portfolios real harm by going against one or all of these truths. They pay higher fees, incur great costs of change, and pay more taxes. They spend hours of time and lots of emotional energy and accumulate "loss leaks" that drain away the results they could have had from their investments if they would only have taken the time and care to understand their own investment realities, developed the sensible long-term program most likely to achieve their real goals, and stayed with it.

The importance of being realistic about investing continues to increase because the markets are increasingly dominated by large, fast-acting, well-informed professionals armed with major advantages. And over the past 20 years, more than four out of five of the pros got beaten by the market averages. For individuals, the grim reality is far worse.

End Notes

1. On Wall Street, the coming of summer is marked with stories about the "summer rally," the fall is heralded by laments about October being the worst month for stocks (statistically, September has been worse), and the turn of the year is celebrated with "the January effect," which doesn't always arrive. Mark Twain's comments about the stock market may have said it best: "October. This is one of the peculiarly dangerous months to speculate in stocks. The others are July, January, September, April, November, May, March, June, December, August, and February" (*Pudd'nhead Wilson*, 1894).
2. Zweig was reporting on research by Javier Estrada.

MR. MARKET AND MR. VALUE

THE STOCK MARKET IS FASCINATING *AND* QUITE DECEPTIVE—
in the short run. Over the very long run the market can be almost boringly reliable and predictable.

Understanding the personalities of two very different characters is vital to a realistic understanding of the stock market and of yourself as an investor. These very different characters are "Mr. Market" and "Mr. Value."

Mr. Market gets all the attention because he's so interesting, while poor old Mr. Value goes about his important work almost totally ignored by investors. It's not fair. Mr. Value does all the work while Mr. Market has all the fun and causes all the trouble.

Introduced in the classic book *The Intelligent Investor*[1] by Benjamin Graham, who also introduced professionalism to investing, Mr. Market occasionally lets his enthusiasms or his fears run wild. Emotionally unstable, Mr. Market sometimes feels euphoric and sees only the favorable factors affecting a business; at other times he feels so depressed that he can see nothing but trouble ahead. To provoke us to action, he keeps changing his prices—sometimes quite rapidly. This most accommodating fellow stands ready, day after day, to buy if we want to sell or to sell if we want to buy. Totally unreliable and quite unpredictable, Mr. Market tries again and again to get us to do something—anything, but at least something. For him, the more activity, the better.

Mr. Market is a mischievous but captivating fellow who persistently teases investors with gimmicks and tricks such as surprising earnings reports, startling dividend announcements, sudden surges of inflation, inspiring presidential pronouncements, grim reports of commodities prices, announcements of amazing new technologies, ugly bankruptcies, and even threats of war. These events come from his big bag of tricks when they are least expected.

Just as magicians use clever deceptions to divert our attention, Mr. Market's very short-term distractions can trick us and confuse our thinking about investments. Mr. Market dances before us without a care in the world. And why not? He has no responsibilities at all. As an economic gigolo, he has only one objective: to be "attractive."

Meanwhile, Mr. Value, a remarkably stolid and consistent fellow, never shows—and seldom stimulates—any emotion. He lives in the cold, hard, real world where there is nary a thought about perceptions or feelings. He works all day and all night inventing, making, and distributing goods and services. His job is to grind it out on the shop floor, at the warehouse, and in the store—day after day, doing the *real* work of the economy. His role may not be emotionally exciting, but it sure is important.

Mr. Value always prevails in the long run. Eventually, Mr. Market's antics—like sand castles on the beach—come to naught. In the real world of business, goods and services are produced and distributed in much the same way and in much the same volume when Mr. Market is "up" as they are when he's "down." Long-term investors need to avoid being shaken or distracted by Mr. Market from their sound long-term policies for achieving favorable long-term results. (Similarly, wise parents of teenagers avoid hearing—or, worse, remembering—too much of what their teen-agers say in moments of stress.)

The daily weather is comparably different from the climate. Weather is about the short run; climate is about the long run—and that makes all the difference. In choosing a climate in which to build a home, we would not be deflected by last week's weather. Similarly, in choosing a long-term investment program, we don't want to be deflected by temporary market conditions.

Investors should ignore that rascal Mr. Market and his constant jumping around. The daily changes in the market are no more important to a long-term investor than the daily weather is to a climatologist or to a family deciding where to make their perma-nent home. Investors who wisely ignore the deceptive tricks of Mr. Market and pay little or no attention to current price changes will look instead at their *real* investments in *real* companies—and to their growing earnings and dividends—and will concentrate on real results over the long term.

Because it's always the surprising short-term events that Mr. Market uses to grab our attention, spark our emotions, and trick us, experienced investors study the details of the stock market's history. Airline pilots spend hours and hours in flight simulators, "flying" through simulated storms and other unusual crises so they are accustomed to all sorts of otherwise stressful cir-cumstances and will be well prepared to remain calm and rational when faced with those situations in real life. Similarly, the more you study market history, the better; the more you know about how securities markets *have* behaved in the past, the more you'll understand their true nature and how they probably *will* behave in the future. Such an understanding enables us to live rationally with markets that would otherwise seem wholly irrational.

At least we would not so often get shaken loose from our long-term strategy by the short-term tricks and deceptions of Mr. Mar-ket's gyrations. Knowing history and understanding its lessons can insulate us from being surprised. Just as a teenage driver is genuinely amazed by his or her all too predictable accidents— "Dad, the guy came out of *nowhere!*"—investors can be surprised by adverse performance caused by "anomalies" and "six sigma events." Actually, those surprises are all within life's normal bell-curve distribution of experiences. For the serious student of markets, they are not truly surprises: Most are really almost actuarial *expectations*, and long-term investors should not overreact. The same goes for pilots. In *The Right Stuff*, Tom Wolfe tells how "unique events" keep causing serious "inexplicable" accidents among test pilots. The young pilots never catch on that these very unusual events are, sadly, an integral part of the dangers inherent in their striving to achieve superior performance.

Of course, most professional investment managers would have good performance—comfortably better than the market averages— *if* they could eliminate a few "disappointing" investments or a few "difficult" periods in the market. (And most teenagers would have fine driving records if they could expunge a few "surprises.") However, the grim reality of life is that most investment managers and most teenage drivers are almost certain to experience "anomalous" events. In investing, these anomalous events occur when an unusual or unanticipated event—ones that the manager understandably sees as quite unexpected and almost certain never to recur in exactly the same way again—suddenly wipes out what otherwise would have been superior investment performance.

The long term *is* inevitable. It is regression to the mean all over again. That's why unusually high stock prices—as much as you may enjoy them—are not really good for you. Eventually, you'll have to give back every single increment of return you get that's above the long-term central trend.

Investing is *not* entertainment—it's a responsibility—and investing is not supposed to be fun or "interesting." It's a continuous process, like refining petroleum or manufacturing cookies, chemicals, or integrated circuits. If anything in the process is "interesting," it's almost surely *wrong*. That's why benign neglect is, for most investors, the secret of long-term success.

The biggest challenge in the stock market is not Mr. Market or Mr. Value. The biggest challenge is neither visible nor measurable; it is hidden in the emotional incapacities of each of us as investors. Investing, like parenting teenagers, benefits from calm, patient persistence and a long-term perspective and constancy to purpose. That's why "know thyself" is the cardinal rule in investing.

The hardest work in investing is not intellectual; it's emotional. Being rational in an emotional environment is not easy, particularly with Mr. Market always trying to trick you into making changes. The hardest work is not figuring out the optimal investment policy; it's sustaining a long-term focus—particularly at market highs or market lows—and staying committed to *your* optimal investment policy.

End Note

1. Benjamin Graham, *The Intelligent Investor* (New York, Harper Collins, 1949).

CHAPTER 4

THE INVESTOR'S DREAM TEAM

THE LARGEST PART OF ANY PORTFOLIO'S TOTAL LONG-TERM returns will come from the simplest investment decision—and by far the easiest to implement: buying the market by investing in index funds. If, like most investors, your instinct is to say, "Oh no! I don't want to settle for average. I want to beat the market!" we may think quietly to ourselves, "Alas, here's another Walter Mitty fantasizing that he'll beat the pros," but we'll still offer you the help you'll need. We'll offer you your investor's dream team.

If you could have anyone—and everyone—you wanted as colleague-investors working with you all day every day, which great investors would you include on your investor's dream team?

Warren Buffett? Done deal. He and his partner Charlie Munger are on *your* team. Peter Lynch? He's yours plus all the analysts and fund managers at Fidelity *and* all the professionals at American Funds or Capital Group. George Soros? Okay! He's on your side too—and so are all the best hedge fund managers across the country. In fact, you can have all the best portfolio managers in the country and all the analysts who work for them on your dream team.

Don't stop there. You can also have all the best analysts on Wall Street—250 at Merrill Lynch, 250 at Goldman Sachs, and 250 at

Morgan Stanley —plus nearly equal numbers at Credit Suisse First Boston, UBS, and Deutsche Bank, *and* all the "boutique" broker analysts specializing in technology or emerging markets.

In fact, you can have *all* the best professionals working for you *all* the time. All you have to do is agree to accept all their best thinking *without* asking questions. (Most of us do the same sort of thing every time we fly: We know that our pilots are trained for and committed to safety. Boring as it may seem, we relax in our seats and leave the flying to the experts.) To get the combined expertise of all these top professionals, all you do is *index*— because an index fund replicates the market, and today's professional-dominated stock market reflects all the accumulated expertise of all those diligent experts making their best current judgments all the time. And as they learn more, they will quickly update their judgments, which means that you will always have the most up-to-date consensus when you index.

Not only do you get the benefits of having the investor's dream team work for you, but you get other important benefits automatically. Peace of mind is one. Most individual investors have to endure regret about their mistakes—and anxiety about potential future regret. Both are unnecessary. And for those who go with the investor's dream team and index, there are several more powerful competitive advantages: lower fees, lower taxes, and lower "operating" expenses. These persistent costs mount up unrelentingly and do as much harm to investment portfolios as termites do to homes. Avoiding them—by investing in index funds—will make you a winner.

Still, accepting the consensus of the experts is not always popular. The pejoratives range from "just settling for average" to "un-American." Hopelessly unpopular with investment managers—and with many hopeful investors—the "market portfolio" or index fund is actually the result of all the hard work being done every day by the investor's dream team. Passive or index investing is seldom given anything like the respect it deserves. But it will, over time, achieve better results than most mutual funds—and far better results than most individual investors achieve.

Considering all the time, cost, and effort devoted to achieving better-than-market results, the index fund certainly produces a lot for very little. This dull workhorse portfolio may appear mindless, but it is in fact based on an extensive body of research about markets and investments that is well worth examining and can be briefly summarized.

The securities market is an open, free, and competitive market in which large numbers of well-informed and price-sensitive professional investors compete skillfully, vigorously, and continuously as both buyers and sellers. Nonexperts can easily retain the services of experts. Prices are quoted widely and promptly. Effective prohibitions against market manipulations are established. And arbitrageurs, traders, hedge funds, market technicians, and longer-term "fundamental" investors continuously seek to find and profit from any market imperfections. Because competing investors are well-informed buyers and sellers—particularly when they are considered in the aggregate—it is unlikely that any one investment manager can regularly obtain profit increments for a large, diversified portfolio through fundamental research because so many other equally dedicated professionals will also be using the best research they can obtain to make their appraisals of whether and when to sell or buy.

Such a market is considered "efficient"—not perfect, and not even perfectly efficient, but sufficiently efficient that wise investors will recognize that they cannot expect to exploit its inefficiencies regularly. The more numerous the skillful competitors are, the less likely it will be that anyone can achieve consistently superior results, and the number of well-educated, highly motivated people going into professional investing has been phenomenal worldwide. In an efficient market, changes in prices follow the pattern described as a "random walk," which means that even close observers of the market will not be able to find patterns in securities prices with which to predict future price changes on which they can make profits.

In a perfectly efficient market, prices not only reflect any information that could be inferred from the historical sequence of prices but also incorporate all that is knowable about the companies whose stocks are being traded. (While there is some specialized evidence that quarterly earnings reports and information on "insider transactions" are not immediately and completely discounted in securities prices, the apparent opportunities to be exploited are so limited that managers of large portfolios would not be able to make effective use of this kind of information anyway.) An efficient market does not mean that stocks will always sell at the "right" price. As everyone knows, markets fluctuate and, as in October 1987 or October–November of 2008, "fluctuation" can be quite violent when fed by collective mistakes such as the exuberant dot-com and subprime-mortgage markets. Investors can be quite wrong in their collective judgments— overly optimistic or overly pessimistic, which will show up in overall market corrections—and can still be highly "efficient" at incorporating into relative market prices any available fundamental information about individual companies.

The beginning of wisdom is to understand that few if any major investment organizations will outperform the market over long periods and that it is *very* difficult to estimate in advance which managers *will* outperform. The next step is to decide whether—even if it *might* be won—this loser's game is ever worth playing.

An index fund provides investment managers and their clients with an easy alternative. They do not have to play the more complex games of equity investing unless they *want* to. The freedom to invest at any time in an index fund is a marvelous freedom of choice because superior knowledge and skill are not consistent attributes of even the best investors. Given the intensity and skill of the competition, superior knowledge is *rare*.

The option to use an index fund enables any investor to keep pace with the market virtually without effort. It allows you to play only when and where and only for so long as you really want to—and to select any part of the wide investment spectrum for deliberate action at any time for as long or as brief a period as you wish. This freedom not to play carries the reciprocal responsibility to yourself to play only for cause and only when the incremental reward fully justifies the incremental risk.

Even our most successful investor, Warren Buffett, recommends that individual investors consider indexing: "Let me add a few thoughts about your own investments. Most investors, both institutional and individual, will find that the best way to own common stocks is through an index fund that charges minimal fees. Those following this path are sure to beat the net results (after fees and expenses) delivered by the great majority of investment professionals."[1]

Active investors *can* do better, and some *will* do better some of the time. But if certain mutual fund managers had been doing significantly better for several years—particularly *after* taxes, fees, expenses, and errors—don't you suppose that with everyone looking, we'd all know which funds they manage?

Investors would be wise to devote attention to understanding the real advantages offered by the market index fund—the product of all the skill and work being done every day by the investor's dream team.

End Note

1. Berkshire Hathaway Annual Report, 1996.

CHAPTER 5

INVESTOR RISK

P OGO, THAT FAVORITE FOLK PHILOSOPHER, SHREWDLY OBSERVED an essential truth that has particular meaning for investors: "We have met the enemy and he is us." So true!

In the same vein, George J. W. Goodman, writing as 'Adam Smith,' wisely explained, "If you don't know who you are, the stock market is an expensive place to find out." We are emotional because we are human. We believe that we'll do better when we try harder. We find it hard to take advice such as, "If it ain't broke, don't fix it." We are not even close to being entirely rational.

For many years, economists assumed that people know what they want to achieve, know how to achieve it, and consistently strive to make rational, unemotional, self-interested decisions in order to achieve their objectives. More recently, behavioral economists have shown that, as human beings, we are not always rational and we do not always act in our own best interests. Here are some of the things we actually do:

- We ignore the "base rate" or normal pattern of experience. (Even though we *know* the odds are against us, we gamble at casinos and get caught up in bull and bear markets.)
- We believe in "hot hands" and winning streaks and believe that recent events matter, even in flipping coins.

- We are overly impressed by short-term results, as in recent mutual fund performance.
- We are "confirmation-biased," looking for and overweighting the significance of data that support our own initial impressions.
- We allow ourselves to use an early idea or fact as a reference point for future decisions even when we know it's "just a number."
- We distort our perceptions of our decisions—almost always in our favor—so that we believe we are better than we really are at making decisions. And we don't learn; we stay overconfident.
- We confuse familiarity with knowledge and understanding.
- As investors, we overreact to good news—and to bad news.
- We think we know more relative to others than we really do. (We also think we are "above average" as car drivers, as dancers, at telling jokes, at evaluating other people, as friends, as parents, and as investors. On average, we also believe our children are above average.)

We now know that as human beings we are endowed with certain inalienable characteristics of mind and behavior that compel us to make imperfect decisions—even dreadfully serious mistakes—as investors.

"At least, let's not do it to ourselves," urged JFK. His caution applies to all investors because we ourselves cause risks that are quite unnecessary and can easily be avoided if we would just recognize our unfortunate proclivities—and discipline ourselves to do no harm, particularly to ourselves and our investments.

Here are some of the investor's risks to avoid:

- *Trying too hard.*
- *Not trying hard enough.* Usually by having too much in money market funds or bonds.

- *Being impatient.* If your investments went up 10 percent a year, that would be less then 1 percent a month. On a *daily* basis, that rate of change would be anything but "interesting." (Test yourself: How often do you check the prices of your stocks? If you check more than once a quarter, you are satisfying your curiosity more than your need for price information.) If you make an investment decision more than once every year or so and are not devoting full time to the market, you are almost surely being too active in trading, and it will cost you.
- *If you invest in mutual funds and Making mutual funds investment changes in less than 10 years.* If you're doing this you're really just "dating." Investing in mutual funds should be *marital*—for richer, for poorer, and so on; mutual fund decisions should be entered into soberly and advisedly and for the truly long term. Changing mutual funds costs investors heavily: The average return realized by mutual fund investors is sharply lower than the returns of the very funds they invest in because investors sell funds with recent disappointing performance and buy funds with recent superior performance. As a result, they sell low and buy high, repeatedly scraping away a significant part of what they could have earned if they had only shown enough patience and persistence.
- *Borrowing too much.* Three out of four of the fortunes that are lost get lost because borrowed money was used. The borrowers were hoping to make an even bigger pile, but it became a painful "pile up" instead.
- *Being naively optimistic.* Being hopeful is almost always helpful in other fields, but in investing it's much better to be objective and realistic.
- *Being proud.* Over and over again studies show that we substantially overestimate our own investment performance relative to the market. And we don't like to recognize and acknowledge our mistakes—even to ourselves. Too often,

we are also stubborn. Remember the adage: "The stock doesn't know you own it." And it doesn't care.

- *Being emotional.* We smile when our stocks go up and frown or kick the cat when our stocks go down. And our feelings get stronger and stronger the more—and the faster—the prices of our stocks rise or fall.

Our internal demons and enemies are pride, fear, greed, exuberance, and anxiety. These are the buttons that Mr. Market most likes to push. If you have them, that rascal will find them. No wonder we are such easy prey for Mr. Market with all his attention-getting tricks.

That's why the best way to start learning how to be a successful investor is to follow the standard instruction: Know thyself. As an investor, your capabilities in two major realms will determine most of your success: your intellectual capabilities and your emotional capabilities.

Your *intellectual capabilities* include your skills in analyzing financial statements (balance sheets, funds flow accounts, and income statements), the extent and accuracy of your ability to store and recall information, how extensively you can correlate and integrate various bits of data and information into insight and understanding, and how much knowledge you can master and use about hundreds of different companies and their stocks.

Your *emotional capabilities* include your ability to be calm and rational despite the chaos and disruptions that will—thanks to Mr. Market—intrude abruptly upon you and your decision making.

Each investor has a zone of competence (the kind of investing for which he or she has real skill) and a zone of confidence (the area of investing in which he or she will be calm and rational). If you know yourself—your strengths *and* weaknesses—you will know the limits you must learn to live within in each realm. The place where your spheres overlap in a Venn diagram (see

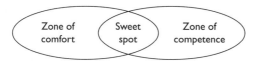

Figure 5.1 Venn diagram

Figure 5.1) is your investor's sweet spot. That's where you want to concentrate: where you have the right skills *and* the right temperament to do your best investing. (In the trade-off between the conflicting investor goals of "eat well" and "sleep well," the sage advice is to "sell down to the sleeping point.") Don't go outside your zone of competence because outside that zone you may get emotional, and being emotional is never good for your investing.

A strong defense is the best foundation for a strong offense in investing, so stay inside your comfort and competence zones. It is *your* money, so treat it with the care and respect it deserves—and you deserve—investing only when you know from experience that you have the requisite skill *and* can be consistently rational.

CHAPTER 6

YOUR UNFAIR COMPETITIVE ADVANTAGE

A LL GREAT STRATEGISTS SEEK TO ESTABLISH A SUSTAINABLE advantage over their competitors. That's why:

- Army generals want to take the high ground and to have the advantage of surprise.
- Coaches want stronger, taller, faster players; strive for ever better conditioning; and care a lot about team spirit and motivation.
- Corporate strategists attempt to create "branding" franchises for their products and services and try to build strong brand loyalty among each group of customers.
- Corporations strive to move up the "experience curve" so that their unit costs of manufacturing will be lower than those of any competitor's. Patent protection, FDA approval, low-cost transportation, technological leadership, consumer preferences, and trademarks all have one thing in common: "competitive advantage."

In each case, strategists are trying to identify and obtain a significant, sustainable, strategic advantage—what competitors will feel is an "unfair" competitive advantage. In investing, there are three ways to achieve a desirable unfair competitive advantage.

The *physically* difficult way to "beat the market" is the most popular, or at least the most widely used. Believers get up earlier in the morning and stay up later at night, and work on weekends. They carry heavier briefcases and read more reports, make and take more phone calls, go to more meetings, and send or receive more e-mails, voice messages, and text messages. They strive physically to do more and work faster in the hope that they can get ahead of the competition.

The *intellectually* difficult approach to beat the market is used by only a few investors, including a very few whose skills inspire us all. They strive to think more deeply and further into the future so that they can gain truly superior insight and understanding of particular investment opportunities.

The *emotionally* difficult approach to superior investing is to maintain calm rationality at all times, never get excited by favorable market events and never get upset by adverse markets. This should be the easiest way. But who among us actually finds it easy to pay *no* attention and sustain that most useful investment stance: benign neglect? That's where personal modesty comes into play and is much needed. You are well-suited to the "easy" way if you can examine the facts of the situation and accept the conclusion that your own efforts are unlikely to improve on a passive acceptance of reality, as we all do with weather conditions and when flying long distances as passengers—and as more investors are learning is wise when investing in today's highly professionalized markets.

The *easy* way to gain—and sustain—an unfair competitive advantage as an investor is to invest through index funds. If you can't beat 'em, join 'em. That's why indexing has become so widely accepted. An even better reason for individuals to index is that you are then free to devote your time and energy to the one role where you have a decisive advantage: knowing yourself and accepting markets as they are—just as we accept weather as it is—to design a long-term portfolio structure or mix of stocks, and perhaps bonds and other investments, that will meet two important tests:

- You can and will live with the market risks of this portfolio.
- The long-term reasonably expectable results will meet your own investment priorities.

While some professional investors are so skillful, so well supported, and so independent that they really can add value by actively changing their investments, the records show over and over again that their number is fewer than most investors want to believe. More important, the chances of your identifying one of the great winners *before* the record has been established is very low.

Changing managers effectively—firing one before disappointment comes *and* hiring a new one before success is shown—is virtually impossible. Such casual "dating" should be recognized as an expensive waste of time and energy and should be avoided by all serious investors.

The great advantage of concentrating on asset-mix decisions is that it helps you avoid the vain search for superior performance. Instead, it focuses your attention on the most important decision in investing—determining the long-term asset mix that will both minimize the odds of unacceptable outcomes caused by avoidable mistakes and maximize the chances of achieving your investment objectives.

If, as the pundits say, "success is getting what you want" and "happiness is wanting what you get," you can be both successful and happy with your investments by concentrating on the asset mix and by living with and investing by a few simple truths, so your investments really will work for and serve you and your purposes. Most individual investors take many, many years, make many mistakes, and go through many unhappy experiences to learn these simple but never easy truths. Fortunately, there is a convenient alternative: As Harry Truman recommended so wisely, we can all learn by reading history. Markets are markets and people are people, and together they have created or written a lot of history.

Here are the "unfair" advantages of index investing in today's market environment:

- Higher rates of return, because over the very long term 85 percent of active managers fall short of the market. And it's nearly impossible to figure out ahead of time which managers will make it into the top 15 percent.
- Lower management fees. Fees of 20 basis points (0.2 percent) or less versus 50 to 60 basis points—year after year.
- Lower operating expenses. Expenses of 5 basis points versus 50 to 75 basis points.
- Lower brokerage commissions because portfolio turnover is a lot less. Commissions under 10 percent per year versus over 100 percent for the average actively managed mutual fund.
- Lower "market impact" because portfolio turnover is so much less.
- Convenience. There are almost no records to keep.
- Lower taxes. Fewer profits are recognized each year— particularly as short-term profits—because turnover is so much lower.
- Freedom from error or blunder, and peace of mind, because no market timing or portfolio strategy decisions and no manager selection decisions are required—decisions that can

so easily go very wrong—and because no single stock ever represents a disproportionate position in your portfolio.

- Freedom to focus on *really* important decisions like investment objectives and sensible long-term investment policies and practices.
- Less anxiety or concern because you never have to worry that you might be making mistakes of omission or commission that will result in unusual losses or missed opportunities.

The case for indexing accumulates greater and greater strength as the period for evaluation lengthens. Performance problems for actively managed funds come episodically. Over the longer term, as more and more people with skill, tenacity, and drive increasingly dominate the markets, those markets surely become more efficient—and trying to beat the market gets harder and harder.

* * * * *

One alternative to index funds may be worth considering: "exchange traded funds" (ETFs). Unlike mutual funds, which are sold and redeemed by the fund company, ETFs are made up of a bundle of stocks tracking a specific stock index trade on an exchange and can be bought or sold through brokers throughout the trading day. ETFs typically have lower expense ratios—0.09 percent for an S&P 500 index ETF versus 0.18 percent for an S&P 500 index fund. However, while there's no charge for buying an index fund, brokerage commissions must be paid to buy ETFs. So if you're a regular, small buyer, go with index funds.

Costs differ greatly quite unnecessarily. Virtually identical index funds have costs that are three times higher—for nothing. For example, Vanguard and Morgan Stanley both offer the classic "commodity" S&P 500 index funds—but the former charges only 0.18 percent while the latter charges a full 0.70 percent for zero benefit. (For every $100,000 invested, Morgan Stanley charges $5,200 more over ten years for nothing.) The same is true for ETFs.

Buyers beware: ETFs also differ significantly in expense ratios, which can range from 0.05 percent to 1.60 percent—an 80 to 1 ratio. Costs are deducted from dividends on the underlying shares with the remainder paid out semiannually. (Dealers make profits on commissions, on securities lending, and on the float between receipt of dividends from underlying companies and semiannual payouts to holders of ETFs.)

For taxable accounts ETFs have a small advantage in tax efficiency because conventional index funds, matching changes made in the composition of the index, incur approximately 2 percent in capital gains each year; ETFs don't adjust their portfolios to match changes in the index. (A few index fund managers offer tax-managed index funds that reduce this already small disadvantage.) The tax benefit can be offset by the higher costs of ETFs due to brokerage commissions.

ETFs have mushroomed, as measured in assets, and proliferated in number and variety since the first one was introduced in 1993. There are now over 1,500 ETFs with assets of nearly $750 billion. Investors should know that most of the growth in ETFs has not come from individual investor demand but from dealers and professionals hedging against particular risks, not investing for the long term.

There are index funds and ETFs for every major market around the world and for small caps or large caps or growth or value— or global: the whole world stock market. However, although each index is designed to replicate the market—or a sector of the market—fairly and accurately, indexes are not all created equal. They differ. Usually the differences are small and inconsequential, but in some markets, differences between indexes—and the index funds that track them—are significant.

* * * * *

A decade ago, Warren Buffett estimated what he considered the annual "horrendous costs" of contemporary active investing to be:

- Over $40 billion—on trading just the shares of Fortune 500 companies—for executing transactions at 6 cents per share.
- $35 billion for management fees, expenses, sales load, wrap fees, and so on.
- $25 billion for a miscellany of spreads on futures and options, costs of variable annuities, and the like.[1]

Noting that all this was "just" 1 percent of the total market value of the Fortune 500, Buffett—always seeing reality as an owner should—reminded us that this $100 billion cut a big chunk out of the $334 billion that the whole Fortune 500 earned in 1998. As a result, investors were earning less than $250 billion—just $2\frac{1}{2}$ percent—on their investment of $10 *trillion*. That $2\frac{1}{2}$ percent return on investment was, in Buffett's view, "slim pickings." Don't we all agree?

Another "leak" in an investor's return comes with taxes driven by portfolio turnover. The more turnover, the more taxes and the lower the accumulated returns. (With short-term gains, which are often realized in mutual funds, the negative impact of taxes is even greater.) The impact of turnover—and of taxes on turnover—is shown starkly in Figure 6.1.

As important as it is, deciding to index or use ETFs is not a *final* decision. Two more decisions must be made: Which index or market and which particular index fund or ETF? If the stock market is somehow distorted—with one or another group of stocks priced with "irrational exuberance" or irrational despair—the index funds replicating that stock market will repeat the distortion. For example, in 2000, the S&P 500 had heavy weightings in several very large-cap stocks that were selling at unsustainably

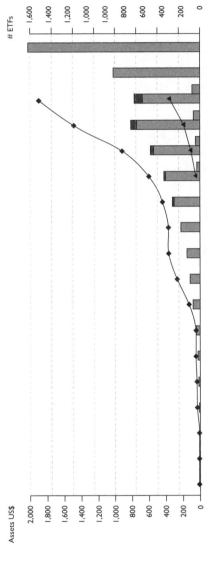

Assets US$

ETFs

	1993	1994	1995	1996	1997	1998	1999	2000	2001	2002	2003	2004	2005	2006	2007	SEP-08	2009-F	2011-F
ETF assets	$0.81	$1.12	$2.30	$5.26	$8.23	$17.60	$39.61	$74.34	$104.80	$141.62	$212.02	$309.80	$412.09	$565.59	$796.70	$764.08	$1,000	$2,000
ETF commodity assets									$0.04	$0.11	$0.32	$0.46	$1.20	$3.38	$6.32	$9.17		
ETF fixed income assets								$0.12	$0.10	$3.97	$5.83	$23.05	$21.32	$5.75	$59.93	$90.77		
ETF equity assets	$0.81	$1.12	$2.30	$5.26	$8.23	$17.60	$39.61	$74.34	$104.66	$137.54	$205.87	$286.28	$389.57	$526.46	$729.89	$664.14		
ETF assets													$15.58	$28.11	$45.87	$8.27		
# ETFs	3	3	4	21	21	31	33	92	202	280	282	336	461	714	1,171	1,499		
# ETPs												23	70	134	268		70	134	268

Source: ETF Research and Implementation Strategy Team, Barclays Global Investors.

Figure 6.1 Nominal Growth of $10,000

49

Pretax rate of return	Annual turnover	Value of $1 million initial investment at the end of 20 years	After-tax rate of return
15%	0	$16,366,500	15.50%
15	3%	14,780,800	14.40
15	10	12,386,300	13.40
15	30	9,694,000	12.00
15	85	8,136,600	11.10
15	100	7,990,800	10.95

Figure 6.2 $1,000,000 initial investment compounded at a 15 percent pretax annual rate of return over a 20-year period, assuming a 27 percent tax rate on all realized gains.

high price/earnings multiples during the Internet euphoria. Predictably, these high flyers returned to earth, bringing down the S&P 500—and bringing equally disappointing results to the index funds that accurately matched the S&P 500.

In this situation, investors had three sensible choices. One choice was a patient "this too shall pass" attitude. The second choice was to invest in a broader "total market" index fund. The third choice was to be somewhat contrarian and invest in an index fund matched to a major area of the stock market that was currently not popular, such as low-P/E "value" stocks. For most investors the middle way—a total market index fund—is often the most sensible choice, particularly if you have no strong reason to be selective in a particular way. And in fact, the middle way performed well after 2000.

If you decide to "overweight" small-cap stocks or emerging markets or even frontier markets in your portfolio structure, you can do so with index funds or ETFs or both. But beware: The argument for index funds is strongest when investing in the most efficient markets like those for large-cap stocks in the United States, United Kingdom, and Japan. Specialized index funds and specialized ETFs invest in markets that are not as broad, deep, and efficiently priced. In smaller markets, market replication is more difficult and less accurate. As you move away from the most efficient markets, you increase the chances that the best research-based active manager will indeed be able to outperform the indexes.

Starting with which market to index is another counterintuitive decision that warrants careful thought. Most investors are surprised to learn that the best "plain vanilla" or "null hypothesis" index fund mix is half *international*. Here's why: Recognizing that diversification is the investor's single "free lunch," it's easy to see that investing proportionately in all the world's major stock markets and all the different economies those markets represent increases diversification significantly.

Investors who decide to concentrate their investments in their home country are making an active decision to emphasize that one country over others. They may be right to do so if their home country has a large, complex, and dynamic economy like the United States and they have large financial obligations or responsibilities in that one country.

But before making such a decision, every investor should at least ponder the reality that most investors in most countries invest mostly in *their* home country. British investors concentrate investments in the United Kingdom. Canadian investors focus on Canada, Japanese investors on Japanese stocks, Australian investors on Aussie stocks, and New Zealanders on Kiwi stocks. Surely, they can't *all* be right all the time even when most of their liabilities and spending responsibilities will be paid in their national currencies. If you woke up to find yourself a New Zealander or German, would you invest mostly in your home country? So why should an American?

To minimize risk relative to return—or to maximize return relative to risk—investors should at least consider fully diversifying internationally. For Americans, this would mean about half our portfolios would be invested outside the United States.

Readers will recognize quickly one of the advantages of indexing: long-term holdings that afford the pleasures of benign neglect. Investors can avoid timing problems—when to change from one market and its index to another—and almost all taxes by the simplest strategy: holding on for the very long term. Of course, this depends on selecting the right index fund at the beginning. That's why wise investors choose an index fund that replicates the broadest market. For fairly rational investors, this will be a broad market index fund in their own country. For very rational investors, this will be a worldwide total market index fund.

End Note

1. *Fortune*, November 22, 1999.

CHAPTER 7

THE PARADOX

A PARADOX IS HAUNTING INVESTMENT MANAGEMENT. THE paradox is that funds with very long-term purposes are not always being managed to achieve long-term objectives that are feasible and worthwhile. Instead, they are being managed to meet short-term objectives that may be neither feasible nor important.

The unimportant and daunting task to which most investment managers devote most of their time with little or no success is trying to "beat the market." Realistically, outperforming the equity market by even close to one-half of 1 percent *consistently*—without taking above-average market risk—would be a great success that almost no sizable investment organizations have achieved for long.[1] Ironically—and painfully for individual investors—institutional investors who strive to *beat* the market almost all come in behind the market indexes.

The truly important but not very difficult task to which investors and their investment managers could and should devote themselves involves four steps:

1. Understanding each investor's real needs
2. Defining realistic investment objectives to meet those realistic needs

3. Establishing the asset mix or portfolio structure best suited to meeting those risk and return objectives
4. Developing well-reasoned investment policies to implement the strategy and achieve the particular investor's realistic long-term investment objectives.

In this work, success can be achieved fairly easily. It is the winner's game—and everyone can be a true winner.

Shifting the asset mix of a 60 percent equity/40 percent fixed-income portfolio to 70:30 may not be a major proposition, but it would likely affect returns more than switching to a new equity manager. If the long-term average rate of return on bonds is 5 percent and the return from investments in common stocks is 9 percent—because there must be a higher long-term rate of return on stocks to persuade investors to accept the risks of equity investing—shifting just 10 percent of the portfolio's assets from bonds to stocks and keeping them there would, over the long term, increase the portfolio's average annual rate of return by four-tenths of 1 percent (4 percent higher return on stock × 10 percent of assets = 0.40 percent). Consistently beating the market rate of return by 0.4 percentage point a year through superior stock selection would be a substantial—and rare—achievement. That's why a change of even such modest magnitude in the basic asset allocation decision can result in an improvement in total return significantly greater than the elusive increment sought in the widespread beat-the-market syndrome.

If the asset mix truly appropriate to the investor's risk and return objectives required an even more substantial emphasis on equities—such as 80:20, 90:10, or even 100:0—the incremental rate of return over the 60:40 portfolio would be even greater: 0.80 percent annually at 80:20 and 1.2 percent annually at 100 percent. Virtually no large investment manager can hope to beat the market consistently by such magnitudes.

Of course, these calculations are mechanical. They present averages, ignoring that actual returns in individual years come in an impressive—and sometimes alarming—distribution of actual annual returns around those averages.

The crucial question is not simply whether long-term returns on common stocks would exceed returns on bonds or T bills *if* the investor held on through the many startling gyrations of the market. The crucial question is whether the investor will in fact hold on for the long term so that the expected average returns can actually be achieved. The problem is not in the market but in ourselves, our perceptions, and our all too human reactions to our perceptions.

This is why it is so important for you to develop a realistic understanding of investing and of capital markets—so Mr. Market will not trick you—and to develop a realistic knowledge of your own tolerance for market fluctuations and your long-term investment objectives—so you won't trick yourself. The more you know about yourself as an investor and the more you understand the securities markets, the more you will know what long-term asset mix is really right for you and the more likely it is that you will be able to ignore Mr. Market and sustain your commitment for the long term.

The real opportunity to achieve superior results lies not in scrambling to outperform the market but in establishing and adhering to appropriate investment policies that enable you to benefit from riding with the main long-term forces in the market. An investment strategy that is wisely formulated with a long-term perspective and clearly defined objectives is the strong foundation on which portfolios should be constructed and managed over time and through market cycles.

In reality, few investors have developed clear investment goals. That's why most investment managers operate without knowing their clients' real objectives and without the discipline of explicit agreement on their mission as investment managers. *This is the investor's fault.*

While investment counseling is more important to long-term success than managing investment portfolios—and could make far more of an economic difference over the long term—most investors will neither do the disciplined work of formulating sound long-term investment policies for themselves nor pay the modest fees that would make counseling sufficiently rewarding for investment managers to provide this much more important service.

Getting it right on investment policy is up to you the investor—after all, it's your money. You know the most about your overall financial and investment situation—your earning power, your ability to save, your obligations for children's educational expenses, the likely timing and scale of needs for spendable funds, and how you feel about the disciplines of investing. Only you know your own tolerance for changes in market prices, particularly at market extremes when investment policies seem least certain and the pressures for change are strongest. So it's your responsibility to know what you really want, and it is your problem. While responsibility for it can be abdicated, responsibility really cannot be delegated.

Each investor should think through his or her own answers to six important questions. (And investment managers would be wise to urge all their clients to do this kind of homework.)

First, what are the real risks to you of an adverse outcome, particularly in the short run? Unacceptable risks should never be taken. For example, it would not make sense to invest all of a high school senior's college tuition savings in the stock market because if the market went down, the student might not be able to pay the tuition bill. Nor would it make sense to invest in stocks all the money saved for a house just two or three years before the intended date of purchase.

Second, what are your probable emotional reactions to an adverse experience? You should know and stay well within your tolerance for interim fluctuations in portfolio value—hopefully, a well-informed tolerance. The emphasis is on *informed tolerance*. Avoiding market risk does have a real "opportunity cost." That's why you should be fully informed of the sorts of increased gains and losses that must be anticipated with each incremental level of market risk taken—and the opportunity cost of each level of market risk *not* taken.

Third, how knowledgeable are you about the history and the realities of investing and the realities and vagaries of financial markets? Investing does not always "make sense"—except in retrospect. Sometimes astute investing seems almost perversely counterintuitive. Lack of knowledge tends to make investors too cautious in bear markets and too confident in bull markets—all too often at considerable cost. Suggestion: Go to your library and spend several hours reading the daily newspapers from the summer and fall of 1929, the fall of 1987, the dot-com era, or the cruel fall of 2008. Getting up close and personal can help you understand how it feels to be in a storm and may help you learn how to remain calm in the next one.

An investor who is well informed about the investment environment will know what to expect. He or she will be able to take in stride the disruptive experiences that may cause other, less informed investors to overreact to either unusually favorable or unusually adverse market experiences.

Fourth, what other capital or income resources do you have, and how important is your portfolio to your *overall* financial position?

Fifth, are there any legal restrictions on your investments? Many trust funds are quite specific. Many endowment funds have restrictions that can be significant, particularly when they spell out how income is to be defined, spent, or both. However, as William Carey and Craig Bright advocated in *The Law and the*

Lore of Endowment Funds (1969), perceived restrictions should be carefully examined because they may not in fact be as confining as they may initially appear.

Sixth, are there any unanticipated consequences of interim fluctuations in portfolio value that might affect your optimal investment policy? We all know that it can be hard for individual investors to continue taking the long-term view when markets are rising rapidly—or, worse, falling rapidly.

Also each of these possible concerns should studied so that the investor can ascertain how much deviation from the normally optimal investment policy—broad diversification at a moderately above-average market risk—is truly warranted. Understanding these insights into the specific investor's situation can provide the realities on which wise investment policies should be developed.

All too few individual investors assert themselves and take up their real responsibilities to themselves and to their families. If investors are not willing to act like principals, we can be sure that the paradox will remain in force for a long, long time. Individual investors have an important opportunity to outperform the averages by achieving the optimal match between their real investment objectives and the long-term investment strategy that's best for each of them.

Observers of the paradox that haunts investment management say it is unrealistic to expect investors to take on the self-discipline of doing all that homework or to expect investment managers to risk straining client relationships by insisting on a well-conceived and carefully articulated investment policy with explicit objectives when investors seem uninterested in going through the discipline.

Escaping from the paradox depends on your asserting your role as the expert on your own needs and resources, and developing appropriate investment goals and policies. For that important work, while we may get some real help, we must look to ourselves.

By redefining the money game, you can focus on what really matters: not the futile struggle to beat the market, but the reasoned and highly achievable goal of setting and meeting your own informed and realistic long-term investment objectives. The more clearly you recognize that others are paying attention to the wrong thing, the more calmly and firmly you can pay attention to the right thing.

End Note

1. One exception is Capital Group Companies, which manages the American Funds family of mutual funds. For a "soup to nuts" description of this unusually professional organization, see my book *Capital*, published by John Wiley & Sons in 2004.

CHAPTER 8

TIME

TIME IS ARCHIMEDES' LEVER IN INVESTING. ARCHIMEDES IS often quoted as saying, "Give me a lever long enough and a place to stand, and I can move the earth." In investing, that lever is *time* (and the place to stand, of course, is on a firm and realistic investment policy).

Time—the length of time investments will be held, the period over which investment results can be measured and judged—is crucial to any successful investment program because it is the key to getting the right asset mix.

Time transforms investments from *least* attractive to *most* attractive—and vice versa—because while the average expected rate of return is not at all affected by time, the range or distribution of *actual* returns around the expected average is greatly affected. Given enough time, investments that might otherwise seem unattractive become highly desirable and vice versa.

The longer the time over which investments are held, the closer the actual returns in a *portfolio* will come to the expected average. The actual returns on *individual* investments, in contrast, will be more and more widely dispersed as the time period lengthens. As a result, time changes the ways in which portfolios of different kinds of investments can best be used by different investors in different situations and with different objectives.

If time is *short*, the highest-return investments—the ones a long-term investor naturally most wants to own—will actually not be desirable, and a wise short-term investor will avoid them. But if the time period for investing is abundantly *long*, a wise investor can commit without great anxiety to investments that in the short run appear very risky.

The conventional time period over which rates of return are usually calculated—their average *and* their distribution—is just one year. While convenient and widely used, this 12-month time frame simply does not match the time periods available to all the different kinds of investors with all their different constraints and purposes. Some investors are investing for only a few days at a time, while others will hold their investments for several decades. The difference in the time horizon matters greatly in investing.

To show how important time is, let's exaggerate for effect and look at the returns expected in a *one-day* investment in common stocks.

If a typical stock's share price is $40, the range of trading during the day might easily be from $39.25 to $40.50—a range of $1.25, or 3.1 percent of the average price for the day. Remembering that the average annual rate of return for common stocks in recent decades has been approximately 10 percent, let's postulate that an investment in this hypothetical stock would have an expected daily return of 0.04 percent (10 percent annual return divided by 250 trading days each year) and a range around that expected average of plus or minus 1.55 percent (the 3.1 percent intraday range divided by 2).

Now let's "annualize" that daily return of 0.04 percent and that daily variation. The average annual expected rate of return would still be 10 percent, but the *range* of returns around the 10 percent would be a daunting ±387.5 percent! In other words, the annualized rate of return for a one-day investment in our hypothetical stock would be somewhere between a *profit* of 405.5 percent and a *loss* of 372.5 percent!

Of course, no sensible investor would knowingly invest in common stocks for only a single day or month or even for a year. Such brief time periods are clearly too short for investments in common stocks because the expectable *variation* in return is too large in comparison to the expected average return. The extra uncertainty incurred when investing in common stocks is not balanced in the very short run by a sufficiently large or sufficiently sure reward. Such short-term holdings in common stocks are not investments; they are rank speculations.

However, this deliberate one-day burlesque of the conventional use of annual rates of return leads to a serious examination of the differences in investor satisfaction when the measurement period is changed. That examination shows why an investor with a very long time horizon might invest entirely in common stocks just as wisely as another investor with a very short time horizon would invest only in Treasury bills or a money market fund. The examination also shows why an intermediate-term investor would, as his or her time horizon is extended outward, shift investment emphasis from money market instruments toward bonds and then more and more substantially toward equities.

Despite the constancy of the average *expected* rate of return— no matter what the time period—the profound impact of time on the actual realized rate of return is clearly demonstrated in the chart in Figure 8.1.

The one-year-at-a-time rates of return on common stocks over the years are almost incoherent. They show both large and small gains and large and small losses occurring in a seemingly random pattern. At best, you could have earned 53.4 percent in a year, but at worst you could have lost 37.3 percent. It seems almost absurd to "summarize" those wildly disparate one-year experiences as having *any* "average" rate of return.

Shifting to five-year periods brings a considerable increase in regularity. There are, for example, few periods with losses, and the periods with gains appear far more often and consistently

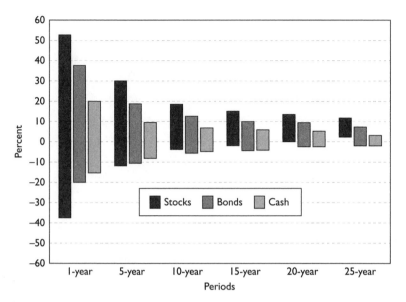

Figure 8.1   Range of returns of stocks, bonds, and cash, after adjusting for inflation (1900–2000).

because, as the measurement period lengthens, the long-term average rate of return increasingly dominates the single-year differences.

Shifting to 10-year periods further increases the consistency of returns. Only *one* 10-year loss is experienced, and most periods show average annual gains of 5 to 15 percent. Again, the power of the average rate of return—now compounded over a full decade—overwhelms the single-year differences.

Moving on to 20-year periods brings even more consistency to the rate of return. There are no losses, only gains. And the gains cluster more closely together around the long-term expected average rate of return.

Appreciating that actual experiences in investing are samples drawn from a continuous stream of experience is vital to understanding the meaning contained in the data. Even in New England, the weather—when considered over a long time—becomes a sensible, reliable *climate* even though the days of bitter cold or sweltering heat seem individually so unpredictable—particularly in regard to the exact dates of their occurrence. Similarly, in investing, the patient observer can see the true underlying patterns that make the seemingly random year-by-year, month-by-month, or day-by-day experiences *not* disconcerting or confusing, but splendidly predictable—on average and over time.

In weather and investments, larger and more numerous samples enable us to come closer and closer to understanding the nature of the normal distribution from which the sample is drawn. This understanding of the normal experience enables you to control your own behavior so that you can take advantage of the dominant normal pattern over the long term and not be thrown off by the confusing daily or even yearly events that present themselves with such force in the short term as Mr. Market gyrates to catch your attention.

The single most important dimension of your investment policy is the asset mix, particularly the ratio of fixed-income investments to equity investments. Analyses of asset mix show over and over again that the trade-off between risk and reward is driven by one key factor: time.

Unfortunately, the time horizon so often used is not chosen for the specific investor but is instead a conventional five years, which usually leads to the familiar recommendation of a 60:40 ratio of equities to debt. A 10-year horizon usually leads to an 80:20 ratio. A 15-year horizon typically results in a 90:10 ratio. And so it goes. The unfortunate reality is that none of these time horizons is "right" for most individual investors who want to provide financial security for their families. They are all far too *short* for an investor with an investment horizon of 20 to 50 years or even more—and most investors will be living—and investing for more than 20 years. It is clear that if more investors used truly long-term thinking, they would invest differently and would earn higher long-term returns.

CHAPTER 9

RETURNS

INVESTMENT RETURNS COME IN TWO VERY DIFFERENT FORMS: quite predictable cash received from interest or dividends and quite *un*predictable—in the short run—gains or losses in market price. Investors who devote most of their time and skill to trying to increase returns by capitalizing on changes in market prices—by outsmarting each other—are making a big mistake.

Changes in market price are caused by changes in the consensus of active investors about what the price of a stock ought to be. This consensus is determined not by individual investors but by thousands of professional investors constantly seeking opportunities for investment profit. To find these opportunities, professional investors:

- Study monetary and fiscal economics and political developments in all the major nations
- Visit hundreds and hundreds of companies; attend thousands of breakfast, lunch, and dinner meetings with corporate executives, economists, industry experts, securities analysts, and other experts
- Study reports and analyses produced by hundreds of companies and dozens of large brokerage firms
- Read extensively in the industry and trade press

- Talk almost constantly on the telephone with people who have ideas, information, or insights with which these active investors might improve their investment performance

In addition to studying the *rational* world, professional investors study the irrational world of "investor psychology," public confidence, politics, and "market tone," because in the short run the markets and market prices—thanks to Mr. Market—are very human and nonrational. The ways in which investors perceive and interpret information and the ways they react to developments have a great impact on market prices, particularly in the short run. Therefore, professional investors are always looking for opportunities to capitalize on changes in other investors' opinions before changes in their own opinions are capitalized on by other investors. Even with all their homework, of course, not all their interpretations and perceptions are correct—some, particularly in retrospect, will seem terribly wrong—but the process of thousands of highly motivated professionals all striving to find the correct prices is so unrelenting and sufficiently skilled that it's very hard to beat.

Investment management in today's dynamic markets is a turbulent, fascinating, hopeful, anguishing, stressful, and sometimes euphoric process of competing in the world's most free, competitive market against many talented and ambitious competitors for advantages gained from greater knowledge, wiser interpretation, and better timing. The irony is that for most investors, professional or individual, most of this activity really does not matter—not because the investment professionals are not highly talented, but because so many competitors are *equally* highly talented.

For all the surface complexity in the process, two main areas are dominant in evaluating common stocks. The first is the consensus of investors on the probable amount and timing of future earnings and dividends. The second is the consensus of investors on the discount rate at which this stream of estimated future dividends and earnings should be capitalized to establish its present value.

Estimates of future dividends and earnings will vary among different investors and at different times because of changes in expectations for long-term growth and cyclical fluctuations in unit demand, prices and taxes, discoveries and inventions, changes in competition at home and abroad, and so forth. Over time, the discount rate considered appropriate will vary with many factors, among which the most important are the perceived risk of the particular investment or investments of its general type and the expected rate of inflation.

The longer the future period over which estimates—of both earnings and dividends and of the discount rate—must be extended, the greater the day-to-day or month-to-month fluctuations in the stock price that will be caused by changes in investors' estimates of present value.

Long-term investors understand from experience the remarkable discipline of the bell curve of economic behavior—the usual distribution of events—and the strong tendency of major forces in the economy and the stock market to move toward "normal." They know that the farther current events are away from the mean at the center of the bell curve, the stronger the forces of reversion, or regression, to the mean, are pulling the current data toward the center.

Mean reversion characterizes the physical world, too. Sailors know the remarkable power of the "righting arm." As a sailboat heels farther and farther over, the keel weight puts increasing force into pulling the hull upright, making it harder and harder to tip even more. While a landlubber may get more and more anxious about tipping over as the sailboat heels farther and farther, an experienced sailor knows that the forces that prevent further heeling are *increasing*. Similarly, the more today's temperature is very hot, the more likely it is that tomorrow's temperature will be *less* hot. And the children of unusually tall people are usually *less* tall.

Investors want to know the most probable investment outlook for the years ahead. One way to look ahead is to appraise the likely *change* in two powerful variables: long-term interest rates and corporate profits. To be realistic, assume that the future range of interest rates and profits will be within the historical upper and lower limits and will tend toward their respective means. (*Caution*: If the market has been going up, investors—who usually evaluate future prospects by looking into the rearview mirror—will add some upward momentum, and if the market has been trending down, they will add some downward momentum. The wise investor will adjust for this unfortunate human tendency.)

Warren Buffett used this straightforward approach near the millennium—when the consensus of investors was that they actually expected nearly 13 percent annual average returns to extend the strong bull market for another 10 years—to show why he expected inflation-adjusted returns of only 4 percent annually.[1] How right he was to be skeptical—again—of the cheery consensus!

Note that the consensus that matters is not today's consensus about the distant future but the consensus that will prevail when we actually get to that distant future. For investment results, as the holding period over which an investor owns an investment lengthens, the importance of the discount factor decreases and the importance of corporate earnings and the dividends paid increases.

For a very long-term *investor*, the relative importance of earnings and the dividends received is overwhelming. For a short-term price *speculator*, everything depends instead on the day-to-day and month-to-month changes in investor psychology and what other people are willing to pay. Like the weather, the average long-term experience in investing is never surprising, but the short-term experience is *constantly* surprising.

The history of returns on investment, as documented in study after study, shows three basic characteristics:

- Common stocks have average returns that are higher than those of bonds. Bonds in turn have higher returns than those of short-term money market instruments.

- The daily, monthly, and yearly fluctuations in actual returns on common stocks exceed the fluctuations in returns on bonds, which in turn exceed the fluctuations in returns on short-term money market instruments.
- The magnitude of the period-to-period fluctuation in rate of return increases as the measurement period is shortened and decreases as the measurement period is lengthened. In other words, rates of return appear more normal over longer periods of time.

While daily, monthly, and annual returns show virtually no predictive or predictable pattern, they are not really random. Hidden within Mr. Market's gyrations is a strong tendency of regression to the mean rate of return. That's why investment managers are learning to describe investment returns in formal statistical terms. Individual investors would be well advised to learn enough about the language of statistics to have an awareness of what is meant by *mean* and *normal distribution* and what is meant by *two standard deviations* as a measure of the frequency with which unusual events are expected to and do occur.

In addition to learning the importance of describing the distribution of returns around the mean, we have learned to separate out the different components in the average rate of return and to analyze each component separately.

There are three main components in the average rate of return:

- The *real* risk-free rate of return.
- A premium over the risk-free rate of return to offset inflation's expected erosion of purchasing power.
- A premium over the inflation-adjusted risk-free rate of return to compensate investors for accepting market risk.

Dividing total returns into these three classes of return makes it possible to compare the returns of each type of investment—stocks, bonds, and Treasury bills. This work has been done in a series of landmark studies by Roger G. Ibbotson and Rex A. Sinquefield. The analysis is informative.

Treasury bills appear quite safe and reliable—in nominal terms, not adjusted for inflation—with apparently positive returns in almost all years. However, when adjusted for inflation, returns are positive just under 60 percent of the time. Even more startling, the average annual rate of return on Treasury bills, after adjusting for inflation, is zero.

In other words, Treasury bills are usually no more than a match for inflation. Most of the time you do get your money back—with its purchasing power intact. But that is all you get. There is virtually no real return *on* your money, just the return *of* your money. (See Figure 9.1.)

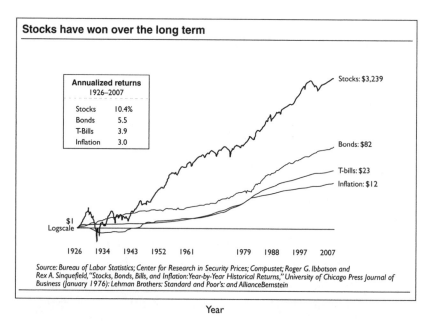

Year

Figure 9.1   Wealth indexes of investments in the U.S. capital markets, 1926–2007

Long-term bonds produce higher returns, inflation-adjusted, for two reasons: Corporate bonds involve a risk of default, and both corporate and government bonds impose on the investor an exposure to market fluctuations caused by their more distant maturity. The market continuously adjusts prices to changing interest rates. Investors don't want to experience the market price fluctuations unless they get a higher rate of return to compensate, so long bonds pay a higher rate of interest—a *maturity premium*. The maturity premium is estimated at 0.9 percent, and the default premium on high-grade long-term corporate bonds works out to about 0.5 percent. Adding these two premiums to the risk-free rate, in normal markets the inflation-adjusted annual real rate of return on long government bonds is a little above 1.0 percent, and on long high-grade corporates it is nearly 1.5 percent.

It makes sense that returns on common stocks are higher than returns on bonds, which guarantee to pay interest and face value at maturity. Stocks make up for not having such guarantees with a risk premium built into their nominal returns. The inflation-adjusted expected real rate of return is about 6 percent.

When the disruptive impact of inflation is removed and returns are examined over reasonably long periods, it becomes clear how consistent investment returns—the returns investors require for their money—really are. This consistency stems from two main factors:

- Investors are sensibly consistent in requiring higher rates of return to compensate them for accepting higher market risk.
- As the period over which returns are measured is lengthened, the short-term volatility in returns caused by fluctuating changes in the discount rate becomes less and less important and the expected dividend stream, which is much more stable, becomes more and more important.

We do not have and cannot hope to get precise or perfectly correct data on rates of return from investments in securities any more than we can expect to get "correct" data by sampling any other complex, dynamic, continuous process that is affected by a multitude of large and small exogenous factors. However, we can get a very useful *approximation* of what returns have actually been and what they are most likely to be, and that is all we really need to establish investment policies for the long term.

Unless you buy in at the start of the period measured, sell out at the end, *and* take your money out of the market, performance data are simply representational statistics. They describe samples from a continuous and very long process in which stock prices go through a "random walk" series of successive approximations of the actual present value of each stock based on continuously revised estimates of future earnings, dividends, and changing discount rates.

Two further propositions on returns are important. First, the impact on returns of changes in the *expected* level of inflation can be enormous, particularly on common stocks, which are virtually perpetual investments. Such a change in the expected rate of inflation from approximately 2 percent in 1960 to approximately 10 percent in 1980 (along with other changes) caused a change in the required nominal average rate of return from common stocks from about 9 percent in 1960 to about 17 percent in 1980, and this produced a major reduction in stock prices. From that reduced level, future returns would meet the returns after inflation that investors needed to justify buying stocks. Note that after adding in the ravages of inflation, the losses investors experienced during that "adjustment" period were the worst in half a century. A decrease in the expected rate of inflation had the opposite effect, as we saw in 1982 and the following 25 years of a bull market rise in prices.

The second proposition on returns is that differences in rates of return that may appear moderate in the short run can, with compounding (because interest is paid not only on the principal but also on the reinvested interest), multiply into very large and quite obvious differences in the long run. (When asked what he considered the human race's most powerful discovery, Albert Einstein allegedly replied without hesitation: "Compound interest!")

Figure 9.2 shows the compounding effect on $1 invested at different interest rates and compounded over different periods of time. It's well worth careful study, particularly to see how powerful time is. That's why the Archimedes' lever of investing is time.

Before leaving the happy realm of investment returns, take another look at Figure 8.1 in Chapter 8, particularly the data on 25-year returns. The moderate levels of *real* returns (adjusted for inflation) are impressive and instructive: 6.6 percent for stocks and 1.8 percent for bonds.

After an extraordinary quarter century of generally highly favorable investment experiences, investors needed to remind themselves in the early years of this century of the normal or "base rate" of investment returns. The high nominal returns of

	Investment period		
Compound rate of return	**5 Years**	**10 Years**	**20 Years**
4%	$1.22	$1.48	$ 2.19
6	1.34	1.79	2.65
8	1.47	2.16	4.66
10	1.61	2.59	6.73
12	1.76	3.11	9.65
14	1.93	3.71	13.74
16	2.10	4.41	19.46
18	2.29	5.23	27.39
20	2.49	6.19	38.34

Figure 9.2 Compound interest over time

the prior quarter century were well above the base rate—as the returns in 2008 would so bluntly prove.

Beware of averages. If stocks return an average of 10 percent per year, how often over the past 75 years did stocks actually return 10 percent? Just *once* (in 1968). And how often did returns even come close to that specific number? Only three times. That's why investors need to "average" delightful and dreadful markets over many years. It's not easy.

The next time you feel excited by a zooming bull market, try to remember what airline pilots say are the two "strong expression" wishes of passengers. The first is the passenger anxious to get to an important meeting, whose plane is on the ground, waiting impatiently for weather to improve, saying, "I wish to God we were in the air flying." The second is the passenger in the air saying, "I wish to God we were on the ground!"

Most investors do not want to preclude themselves arbitrarily from making the big score—the opportunity to "shoot the lights out."[2] If you believe with Louis Pasteur that "chance favors the prepared mind," be sure that you are prepared. First, be prepared to find nothing much. In nearly 50 years of continuous active involvement with many of the world's best investors, I've found only two major opportunities that weren't obvious to many others. That's discovery at a rate of only once every 25 years of nearly full-time searching.

If you find a great investment opportunity, what should you do? Try asking four questions and then ask other people to examine your reasoning process with you:

1. What could go really *right*, and how likely is it?
2. What could go *wrong*, and how likely is that?
3. Am I so confident that I plan to invest a significant part of my portfolio in this one?
4. If the price goes down, will I *really* want to buy a lot more?

End Notes

1. *Fortune*, November 22, 1999
2. My father loved bridge and played often. He was impressed one evening when, after three passes, his bridge partner opened with a preemptive bid: "Small slam in hearts!" He was astonished when his happy partner said, "It's a laydown!" Dad was astounded as his partner showed his hand: It was all hearts! Aghast, Dad asked the obvious question, "Why didn't you bid *grand* slam?" He was not amused by the reply: "Because you had not bid, I wasn't sure how much support your hand would give me." Dad never fully recovered. The opportunity missed was too great to forget.

CHAPTER 10

INVESTMENT RISKS

R*ISK IS SUCH A SIMPLE LITTLE WORD THAT IT IS AMAZING* how many different meanings are given to it by different users.

Risk is different from uncertainty. *Risk* describes the expected payoffs when their probabilities of occurrence are *known*. Actuarial mortality tables are a familiar example. The actuary does *not* know what will happen in 14 years to Mr. Frank Smith but does know quite precisely what to expect for a group of 100 million people as a group—in each and every year. "Riskiness" in investing, by contrast, is akin to *uncertainty*, and that's what the academics mean when they discuss beta (relative volatility) and market risk. Too bad they don't use the exact terms. Risk is not having the money you need when you need it.

Risk is both in the markets and in the individual investor. Some of us can live comfortably with near-term market volatilities—or, at least, resist the primal urge to take action—knowing that over the long run, more market volatility usually comes with higher average returns.

Active investors typically think of risk in four different ways. One is "price risk": You can lose money by buying stock at too high a price. If you think a stock might be high, you *know* you are taking price risk.

The second type of risk is "interest rate risk": If interest rates go up more than was previously expected and are already discounted in the market, your stocks will go down. You'll find out that you were taking interest-rate risk.

The third type of risk is "business risk." The company may blunder, and earnings may not materialize. If this occurs, the stock will drop. Again, you were taking business risk.

The fourth way is the most extreme, "failure risk." The company may fail completely. That's what happened with Penn Central, Enron, WorldCom, and Polaroid. As the old pros will tell you, "Now *that* is *risk!*" And that's why we should all diversify.

Real risk is simple: not enough cash when money is really needed—like running out of gas in the desert. The old pros wisely focus on the grave risk all investors—and 401(k) investors in particular—should focus on: running out of money, particularly too late in life to go back to work.

Another way to look at risk has come from the extensive academic research done over the past half century. More and more investment managers and clients are using it because there's nothing as powerful as a theory that works. Here's the concept: Investors are exposed to three kinds of "investment risk." One kind of risk simply cannot be avoided, so investors are rewarded for taking it. Two other kinds of risk *can* be avoided or even eliminated, so investors are *not* rewarded for accepting these unnecessary and avoidable kinds of risk.

The risk that cannot be avoided is the risk inherent in the overall market. This market risk pervades all investments. It can be increased by selecting volatile securities or by using leverage—borrowed money—and it can be decreased by selecting securities with low volatility or by keeping part of a portfolio in cash equivalents. But it cannot be avoided or eliminated. It is always there. Therefore, it must be *managed*.

The two kinds of risk that can be avoided or eliminated are closely associated. One involves the risk linked to individual securities; the other involves the risk that is common to each type or group of securities. The first can be called "individual-stock risk," and the second can be called "stock-group risk."[1]

Few examples will clarify the meaning of stock-group risk. Growth stocks as a group will move up and down in price in part because of changes in investor confidence and willingness to look more or less distantly into the future for growth. (When investors are highly confident, they will look far into the future when evaluating growth stocks.) Interest-sensitive issues such as utility and bank stocks will all be affected by changes in expected interest rates. Stocks in the same industry—autos, retailers, computers, and so forth—will share market price behavior driven by changing expectations for their industry as a whole. The number of common causes that affect groups of stocks is great, and most stocks belong simultaneously to several different groups. To avoid unnecessary complexity and to avoid triviality, investors usually focus their thinking on only major forms of stock-group risk.

The central fact about both stock-group risk and individual-stock risk is this: They *do not need to be accepted* by investors. They can be eliminated. Unlike the risk of the overall market, risk that comes from investing in particular market segments or specific issues can be diversified away—all the way to oblivion.

That's why, in an efficient market, no incremental reward can or will be earned over the market rate of return simply by taking either more individual-stock risk or more stock-group risk. Either type of risk should be incurred only when doing so will enable the investor to make an investment that will achieve truly worthwhile increases in returns. The evidence is overwhelming that, while enticing, such ventures are usually not sufficiently rewarding. Yes, professional investors often are quoted as being "overweighted" in one group or another, but the fact that this is being done does not mean it is, on average, successful.

The lack of reward for taking individual-stock risk or stock-group risk is important. An investor who takes such risks can hope to be rewarded only by superior skill—relative to the aggregate skill of all competing investment managers—in selecting individual stocks or groups of stocks that were somehow inappropriately priced. As is explained in Chapter 2, an investor who takes these risks can profit only if his or her competitors make mistakes—not an encouraging basis for making a major commitment.

Clearly, such risks can be avoided by using the simple and convenient strategy of investing in an index fund—a portfolio that replicates the market. No deviations in portfolio composition relative to the overall market means no deviations in rate of return and no stock-group risk or individual-stock risk. An index fund provides a convenient and inexpensive way to invest in equities with the riskiness of particular market segments and specific issues diversified away.

Note that eliminating these two particular forms of risk does not mean that all risk is gone. Overall market risk will always be there, and in the field of risk, that's the big one. Figure 10.1 shows vividly how the riskiness of a single stock consists primarily of specific-issue risk and market-segment risk but also shows that in a typical portfolio these two kinds of risk—after diversification—are only a small part of the investor's total risk.

The figure also shows that the typical investor with several different mutual funds will have even more diversification and that this degree of diversification will further reduce the specific-issue and market-segment risks to a very small percentage of total risk. (Index fund investors who add international index funds clearly get still more diversification.)

Risk-averse investors are willing to accept lower rates of return if they can reduce the market risks they *must* take in investing. And they are willing to see other investors get higher rates of return as an inducement to accept a larger share of the unavoidable market risk. But they will not pay other investors to take risks that can easily be avoided altogether by "buying the market," or indexing.

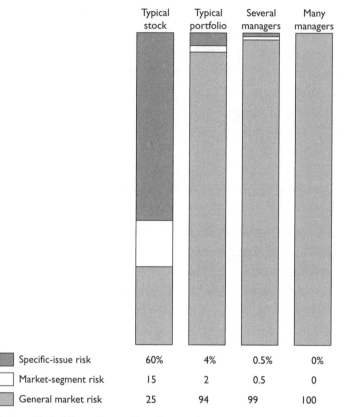

		Typical stock	Typical portfolio	Several managers	Many managers
■	Specific-issue risk	60%	4%	0.5%	0%
□	Market-segment risk	15	2	0.5	0
▣	General market risk	25	94	99	100

Figure 10.1 How diversification reduces nonmarket risk

The optimal level of market risk for a very long-term investor is moderately above the average. This level makes sense because many other investors are not free to take a very long-term view; their investments will be liquidated sooner—for their children's education, at the termination of a trust, or for a host of other near- to medium-term events for which plans must be made. Other investors are simply unable to look with calm forbearance on the abrupt and substantial day-to-day, month-to-month, and year-to-year changes in stock prices that will be experienced in an equity portfolio over the long term. These investors want less risk and less fluctuation and are willing to pay a price—by giving up some incremental return—to get what they want.

In summary, the total return to an equity investor has four components:

1. The risk-free return after absorbing expected inflation
2. An extra return to compensate for the riskiness or price uncertainty of investing in the overall equity market
3. A potential extra return for investing in one or more particular groups of stocks or market segments that for various economic, business, or market psychology reasons may behave differently from the overall market
4. A potential extra return for investing in specific stocks that, for the same sorts of reasons, may behave differently from the overall market

Corresponding to each component of *return* is a component of *risk*.

In investment management, we now know that the crucial factor is not how to manage rates of return but how to manage market risk. By managing market risk, we are doing two things at the same time:

1. Deciding deliberately what level of market risk to establish as the portfolio's basic policy
2. Holding to that chosen level of market risk through good and bad markets.

Changes in the level of market risk should be made only because the investor's long-term objectives have changed.

That managing market risk is the primary objective of investment management is a profound assertion. It is the core idea of this chapter. The rate of return obtained in an investment portfolio comes from three sources, in this order of importance: first and foremost, the level of market risk assumed—or avoided—in the portfolio; next, the consistency with which that risk level is maintained through market cycles; and last, the skill with which specific-stock risk and stock-group risk are eliminated or minimized through portfolio diversification *or* are well rewarded when deliberately taken.

The difference between true investment risk and apparent riskiness or market risk is a function of time. Yes, stocks can be very risky if time is short. But unless you begin your investment program at a silly "too high" level in the stock market, when the time is long enough, the apparent riskiness of stocks evaporates and the favorable long-term returns become increasingly evident, as shown in Figures 10.2a, b, c, and d. If you're not confident that the market is low, you'll be wise to use dollar-cost averaging (investing a fixed dollar amount at regular intervals) to get invested gradually.

For investors, investment risk can also be divided by *time* into "short-term risk" and "long-term risk." The real risk in the short term is that you will need to sell—to raise cash—when the market happens to be low. That's why, in the *long* term, the risks are clearly *lowest* for stocks, but in the *short* term, the risks are just as clearly *highest* for stocks. One risk that most investors are not prepared for, however, is *how long* it can take for the stock market to recover to peak prices. It's worth remembering that it took 16 years for the S&P 500 stock index to get back up to its 1966 peak and even longer to regain the peak of 1929. But if you do not need to sell and don't sell, you really shouldn't much care about the nominal fluctuations of stock prices. They may be interesting, but they aren't any more relevant to you than is stormy weather in faraway places or low tide on the high seas.

Since the real risks in the long run are the risks of inflation and the risks created—unnecessarily—by investors, the investor's

Stock returns have been volatile over the short term

S&P 500: annual returns

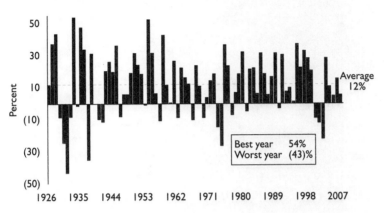

a

Five-year losses have been rare

S&P 500: Rolling five-year periods (annualized)

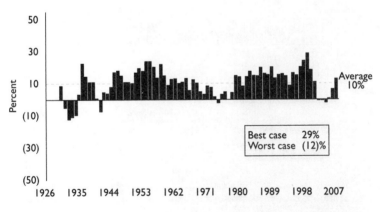

b

Figure 10.2a, b The longer you hold stocks, the less your risk and the surer your gain.

Source: Courtesy of Alliance Bernstein

Ten-year losses have been very rare

S&P 500: Rolling ten-year periods (annualized)

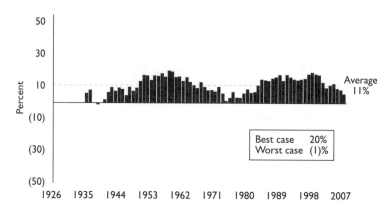

c

Stocks have not lost money over the long term

S&P 500: rolling periods (annualized)

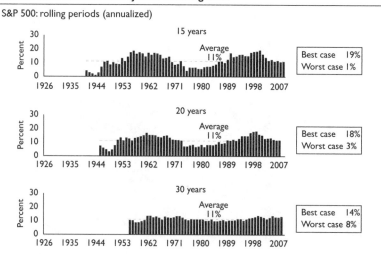

d

Figure 10.2c, d The longer you hold stocks, the less your risk and the surer your gain.

Source: Courtesy of Alliance Bernstein

best answer to short-term market riskiness is to ignore the interim fluctuations and be a long-term investor.

Risk tolerance does not describe the behavior we expect of ourselves when we calmly consider normal markets or long-term averages or normal volatility of returns. Risk tolerance anticipates our behavior when we are driven by real worries during market extremes, particularly after we've recently been proven wrong—again. To the extent that you know that your investments will be held for the very long term, you have automatically self-insured against the uncertainty of short-term market price fluctuations, because as long as you stay invested, the price fluctuations of Mr. Market just won't matter to you.

Recognition that investment risk drives returns instead of being simply a residual of the struggle for higher returns transforms the concept of investment policy. We now know to focus not on rate of return but on the informed management of risk.

End Note

1. Academic writers use slightly different terms to describe these three types of risk: Market risk is called "systematic risk," individual-stock risk is called "specific risk," and stock-group risk is called "extra market risk". The terms used here seem clearer and more natural. Risk identified as either individual-stock risk or stock-group risk is the risk that the price of an individual stock or group of stocks will behave differently from the way the overall market will behave—either favorably or unfavorably—over the period in which investment returns are measured.

CHAPTER 11

BUILDING PORTFOLIOS

WHETHER INVESTING IS PRIMARILY AN ART OR A SCIENCE HAS long been a favorite topic of informal discussion among professional investment managers, perhaps because the discussions typically are resolved quite cheerfully by demonstrating that since the practice of investing is clearly not a science, it therefore must be an art.

Anyone who has observed gifted investors at work will recognize the art—subtle, intuitive, complex, and usually inexplicable—in selecting individual stocks or groups of stocks. The few great artists are true heroes of the profession who add value to portfolios by seeing and seizing opportunities others miss or recognize only later.

However, for most investment managers, portfolio management is neither an art nor a science. It is instead an unusual problem in engineering, determining the most reliable and efficient way to reach a specified goal, given a set of policy constraints, and working within a remarkably uncertain, probabilistic, always changing world of partial information and *mis*information, all filtered through the inexact screen of human interpretation.

While certainly far from perfect, recent advances in the availability of data and the development of modern portfolio theory are providing investment managers—and their more sophisticated clients—with the tools and concepts they need to understand and define the investment problem so that it can be managed. (It would be a naive presumption to believe that the problems of managing an investment portfolio can be "solved." We must be willing to live with the problems being brought under only partial control and being managed to an approximate standard of performance.)

As was explained in Chapter 10, we now know that the real challenge in long-term investing is not how *to increase returns*—by buying low and selling high—but how *to manage risk* by deliberately taking appropriate market risks that will lead over time to moderately increased returns.

The great lesson of engineering is that the key to finding the solution is to define the real problem correctly. When you have defined the problem correctly, you are well on your way to finding the correct solution. In investing, which of these is *your* real problem: How to invest for the next 10, 20, or 30 *years* or how to invest for the next 10, 20, or 30 weeks? If your real problem is investing for the longer term, you'll want to ask yourself: Is your current "solution" truly long term?

Portfolio management is investment engineering. Good portfolio design eliminates avoidable and unintended risk and maximizes expected returns at a deliberately chosen level of market risk—producing an *efficient* portfolio. An efficient portfolio has greater expected returns than any other feasible portfolio with equal risk—and less risk than any other feasible portfolio with equal expected returns.

Once an efficient portfolio has been constructed at the level of risk that is appropriate for a particular investor, it would not make sense to incur more individual-stock risk or stock-group risk unless such risk is directly associated with a specific opportunity to capture sufficient extra return.

The amount by which market risk and return can be magnified in a portfolio by investing in moderately higher-market-risk, more price-volatile stocks is not spectacular, but the benefits over the very long run can be worthwhile. A portfolio with a market risk that is 20 percent greater than the overall market average is feasible. A market risk much higher than that would be difficult to design into a portfolio while keeping the portfolio well diversified. The number and variety of stocks needed to achieve good diversification *and* provide that much additional market risk are simply not available in the market.

The expected "extra" rate of return for a portfolio with 20 percent more than average market risk would be, on average and over the very long term, 1.2 percentage points annually.[1] If 1.2 percentage points of incremental return over the market average return seems modest, remember that *no* sizable mutual fund has achieved that amount of annual incremental return over any sustained period!

Thus far, our discussion has concentrated on equity investments. Portfolio management for bonds is different in the details, but the main concepts are much the same. Like stocks, bonds present both individual-bond risk and group risk that can and should be diversified away. For example, bonds issued by companies in a particular industry will, as a group, change in value with major changes in that industry's economics. Bonds sharing particular call or refunding features will rise and fall as a group in relative market popularity. The normal difference in yield (and therefore price) between corporate and government bonds changes, causing larger or smaller spreads between corporates as a group and governments as a group.

Bond rating agencies have found that most of their rating errors are caused by the difficulty inherent in estimating such group risks, not in estimating the individual risk of a particular issuer compared to other issuers in the same industry or group. Sadly, this was proven again in 2008 when AAA credit ratings were given to newly issued securities backed by subprime mortgages.

The rating agencies were seriously wrong *systematically* on group risk, which led to enormous losses for investors relying on Moody's and S&P ratings. This has happened before—starting with AAA street railways in the 1920s.

Conceptually, bond portfolio management starts with a passive portfolio that represents the overall bond market. This baseline portfolio is diversified across numerous groups and across individual issues to protect against the credit risk of individual issuers or types of issuers, and it uses an evenly spaced schedule of maturities to defend against adverse changes in interest rates.

As with equities, the historical evidence is that the risk of individual bonds can be substantially eliminated through diversification. Portfolios of medium- to lower-grade issues do, after absorbing all actual losses through defaults, provide higher net returns over time than portfolios of higher-grade issues. That's why portfolio managers with direct access to superb credit research can increase risk-adjusted returns while concentrating on mispricing among medium- to lower-grade bonds.

Individual investors should never buy individual corporate bonds: Diversification is an absolute necessity in bond investing to ensure the return of your money. Fortunately, well-managed bond funds of all types are now available at low cost. How much and whether to invest in bonds at all, not which particular bonds you invest in, will be the most powerful determinant of your overall results.

As it has been for fiduciaries since the invention of insurance and pooled risk accounts in merchant shipping on sailing vessels hundreds of years ago, the basic responsibility of mutual fund managers and all financial service professionals is to prevent surprises and control portfolio risk in deliberate pursuit of wisely determined and explicitly stated long-term investment objectives. Even though most investors see their work as active, assertive, and on the offensive, the reality is and should be that stock investing and bond investing are primarily *defensive* processes.

The great secret of success in long-term investing is avoiding serious, permanent loss. The saddest chapters in the long history of investing are tales about investors who suffered serious losses they brought on themselves by trying too hard or by succumbing to greed. Leverage is all too often the instrument of self-destruction. Investors will be wise to remember the great difference between *maximization* and *optimization* as they decide on their long-term strategy. Icarus was a maximizer, as were many of history's destroyed "fortune builders" who, like Hamlet's hapless military schemer, were hoisted with their own petards.[2]

End Notes

1. 20 percent × 6 percent return on equities over and above the risk-free rate of return = 1.2 percent incremental return.
2. A petard was a small bomb.

CHAPTER 12

WHY POLICY MATTERS

THE PRINCIPAL REASON YOU SHOULD ARTICULATE YOUR LONG-term investment policies explicitly and in writing is to protect your portfolio from yourself—helping you adhere to long-term policy when Mr. Market makes current markets most distressing and your long-term investment policy suddenly seems most seriously in doubt.

Technology has transformed investing just as GPS (global position system) technology has transformed navigation. Thanks to new technology, investment managers can produce—within the array of feasible results—the intended long-term "relative-to-market" outcome for any particular portfolio. Investors now have every right to expect results that match their reasonable expectations—and their fund managers' promises. At least as important, investors are now free to focus on developing explicit long-term investment policies that will achieve specified goals persistently within their own tolerance for interim market risk.

The best shields against Mr. Market's short-term data and distress are knowledge and understanding, particularly of yourself and your own goals and priorities. That's why your carefully considered investment strategy should be committed to writing. Don't trust yourself to be completely rational when those all around you are driven by emotion. You are human too.

Misdemeanors in investing are almost all the result of investors' inadequate advance understanding of the *internal* realm of their own short-term emotions and their long-term objectives or the *external* realm of capital markets and investments—or both. All too often investment policy is both vague and implicit, left to be "resolved" only in haste when unusually distressing market conditions are putting the pressure on and when it is all too easy to make the wrong decision at the wrong time for the wrong reasons.

Such hasty reviews typically result in investors selling stocks *after* they have dropped steeply in value—to buy into bonds and other fixed-income investments that will not rise as rapidly as stocks in the next cycle of the equity market—and vice versa: buying stocks at or near the market's high when the record looks most compelling. Clearly, such ill-timed changes in the asset mix—selling low and then buying high—can be severely harmful to your long-term returns.

We may be able to see that in theory our long-term interests are best served by lower stock prices, so we can all buy at bargain prices. But who among us can honestly say that he or she is delighted by falling markets? And who does not feel a warm glow of affection for stocks and markets that have gone up, even though we know it means that stocks are now more expensive to buy and future rates of return on additional investments at these price levels will surely be lower?

By contrast, who among us would close our pocketbook and turn away from the store that puts its most attractive wares on sale at 10, 20, or even 30 percent off its recent prices? None of us would say, "I don't want to buy these things when they're on sale; I'll wait until the price goes back up and buy then." But that's exactly how most of us behave toward investments.

When the market drops—putting stocks "on sale"—we stop buying. In fact, the records show that we even join in the selling.

And when the market rises, we buy more and more enthusiastically. As Jason Zweig of *Money* magazine puts it, "If we shopped for stocks the way we shop for socks, we'd be better off." We are wrong when we feel good about stocks having gone up, and we are wrong when we feel bad about stocks having gone down. A falling stock market is the necessary first step to buying low.

Psychologists who study anxiety and fear have found that four characteristics make people more worried about the perceived riskiness of a situation than the realities would warrant: large-scale consequences, the lack of personal control or influence, unfamiliarity, and sudden occurrence. As a result, we are more fearful of air travel (in which, in a typical year, fewer than 30 people are killed and far fewer than 350 are hurt) than of travel in cars (in which 45,000 people are killed yearly in the United States, and well over 350,000 are injured).

Most investors experience great anxiety over large-scale, sudden losses in portfolio value primarily because they have not been informed in advance that such events are how markets sometimes behave. Sharp losses are to be expected and even considered *normal* by those who have studied and understand the long history of stock markets.

Such drops in the market are—with a good understanding of market history—nearly predictable, not in their timing but in their magnitude and suddenness. No wonder nonstudents experience attacks of anxiety. And it is in these periods of anxiety—when the market has been most severely negative—that investors predictably engage in ad hoc "reappraisals" of long-term investment judgment and allow their short-term fears to overwhelm the calm rationality of long-term investing.

Investors need protection from their human proclivities toward unrealistic hopes and unnecessary fears, provoked by the emotionally compelling experiences of positive or negative surges in the market and by the current opinions that drive them. This is understandable; investors who are not sufficiently informed about the true nature of investment markets do get surprised. Severe storms such as the financial world experienced in 2008 surprise almost everyone. And their reactions to surprise in turn resurprise almost everyone else.

Investors can get inundated by information in written reports from economists and stock analysts and by telephone calls and e-mails on market transactions that give a compelling urgency to the here and now—and to what others are or may be thinking of doing. The resulting excessive attention to the present and the immediate future not only produces "group think" errors, but it also distracts our attention from careful study of the profound difference between the short-run nature and the long-run nature of investments.

You can substantially improve your long-term investment returns by being sure that you understand the realities of the investment environment in which your portfolio will operate. Thoughtful, objective study of the past is the best—and least costly—way to develop an understanding of the basic nature of markets. That's why it pays to study the rates of return and patterns of deviation from the averages over the past several decades, learning as thoroughly as possible why markets move as they do.

As an investor, it is more rewarding to study investment history than to study the present—or various estimates of the future—so you won't get caught in Santayana's trap: "Those who cannot remember the past are condemned to repeat it." Again, visit your local library and read the financial section of your favorite magazine or newspaper for 1973, 1987, 1962, 1928–29, 1957, 2000, and 2008. As Yogi Berra said, "It's déjà vu all over again." Markets always have been and always will be surprising because every market is "different" in its details. But the major characteristics of markets are remarkably similar over time.

Only by understanding the nature of investing and capital markets will you escape the paradox in which little or no attention is devoted to the truly important work of developing and adhering to wise, appropriate investment policies and practices that can, over time, achieve better results for you than most investors enjoy or suffer.

As an investor, you will be winning when the results you get are the results you want. They are brought to you by your following the long-term policies you chose that match your personal long-term priorities.

CHAPTER 13

THE WINNER'S GAME

THE WINNER'S GAME IN INVESTING—OPEN TO *ALL* INVESTORS, so *every* investor can be a real winner—is almost easy. Almost. The first secret for success is that each investor has to ignore the "beat the market" hype that pervades the advertising that floods out of stockbrokers, "performance" mutual funds, and the investment letters from stock market gurus—all working with Mr. Market.

The second secret for success is that each investor must decide for himself or herself what investment policy will, over the long term, have the best chance of producing the particular results he or she most wants to achieve. These winning investors are not in competition with each other; they are in competition only with themselves. Can they stay "on mission"—even when Mr. Market goes into his gyrations?

While most investors think of investing as a conventionally blended complex of activities, it is easy and worthwhile to unbundle investing into five *separate* levels of decisions for each investor to make:

- *Level One.* Settling on your long-term objectives and asset mix—the optimal proportion of equities, bonds, and perhaps other assets to achieve those objectives.

- *Level Two.* Equity mix, the proportions in various types of stocks—growth versus value, large cap versus small cap, domestic versus international. If you have a large portfolio, the same decisions can be made on subcategories for each major asset class.
- *Level Three.* Active versus passive management—the method chosen for implementation of your mix of investments. For most investors, passive index funds will be the best long-term choice.
- *Level Four.* Specific fund selection (where most investors unfortunately concentrate almost all their time and effort)—deciding which mutual funds will manage each component of the overall portfolio.
- *Level Five.* Active portfolio management—selecting specific securities and executing transactions.

The least costly *and* the most valuable decisions are on level one: getting it basically right on long-term goals and the asset mix. The last two levels—the active management of mutual funds and active management of portfolios (buying and selling specific securities)—are the most expensive and the least likely to add value. (In addition, taxes as well as operating costs are much higher with the activity of trying harder.)

That's the ultimate irony of the loser's game: We can be, and all too often are, dazzled by the excitement and the action and the "chance to win" on level five—Mr. Market's favorite territory—where the costs to play are so high and the rewards are so small. Even worse, the search for ways to beat the market distracts us from focusing on level one, where the costs are low and the rewards can be large.

Investment policy is the explicit linkage between your long-term investment objectives and the daily work of investing. If policy is not determined through carefully developed understanding, it *will* be determined by anecdotal "adhocracy." Portfolio operations should clearly be the responsibility of the fund manager, but selecting the right fund is your responsibility as an investor—and your opportunity.

Since almost any asset mix can be achieved through low-cost indexing, investors considering active management should have an objective basis for deciding that the actual incremental returns—not just the promises—will fully justify the cost and risk of selecting active managers.

If, instead of using index funds, you do wish to select an investment manager who deliberately differentiates his portfolios from the market, you must take the time to understand clearly *how* he will differentiate his portfolios (whether by betting heavily on a few stocks, for example, or by favoring a particular stock market sector); *when* he will do so (whether continually as part of a long-term strategy or occasionally as a short-term tactic); and, most importantly, *why* he is confident that he will achieve favorable incremental results by taking these actions. If you're thinking of making these exceedingly difficult decisions yourself as an individual investor, please think again. In the investment school of hard knocks, the tuition is too high and the benefits too low.

Setting an explicit policy on market risk is easier said than done. In measuring investment performance, we have good tools, but we do not have precision instruments.

Time, as we have seen, is the single most important factor that separates the appropriate investment objective of one portfolio from the appropriate objective of another portfolio. The key is the length of time over which the portfolio can and will remain committed to a sustained investment policy and over which you will patiently evaluate investment results versus your objectives and policies.

Liquidity need not be given separate consideration in a well-diversified portfolio *provided* the portfolio is invested in the kinds of securities appropriate to its time horizon. Many investors wisely want to have a reserve for current spending—a "cushion for caution" to separate their long-term investment portfolios from their regular expenses so that they can and will sustain long-term commitments to their long-term advantage. The amount of this dedicated reserve should be carefully determined and not be allowed to influence the long-term investment portfolio. Cash positions *within the investment portfolio* should be minimized and most likely be kept at zero.

Of great concern is that many young 401(k) investors keep large proportions of their portfolios in money market or "stable value" funds, even though they may be decades away from retirement. They are *saving*, but they are not *investing*—as they really must to assure themselves of adequate retirement security.

Income requirements are excluded from this discussion of investment policy because the rate of return for an investment portfolio cannot be increased just because you want more money to spend. It is indeed a curious idea that the investment objective for a portfolio can or even should be set according to the funds the investor wants to spend each year. Sometimes this idea shows up in pension funds where the actuarial assumption about the rate of return is put forth as a "guide" to investment management. Sometimes it shows up when college presidents insist on higher endowment fund income to make up for operating deficits. And sometimes it arises when individuals try to force their retirement funds to finance a more expensive way of life than the funds can sustain.

In all its forms this practice is nonsense. Instead of spending decisions influencing investment decisions, it must be the other way around. Spending decisions should most definitely be governed by investment results—which follow from investment policies and the market's returns—because, frankly, the market doesn't give a damn what you *want* to spend.

From time to time, perhaps once every two or three years, a systematic examination of your needs and objectives, your market experience, and your investment policy is appropriate.

Here are a few simple tests of investment policy:

1. Is the policy realistically designed to meet your real needs and objectives as a long-term investor?
2. Is the policy written so clearly and explicitly that a competent stranger could manage the portfolio and conform to your true intentions?
3. Would you have been able to sustain a commitment to the policies during the most troubling markets that have actually been experienced over each of the past 50 years—including 2008?
4. Would the policy, if implemented, have achieved your long-term objectives?

Sound investment policies will meet *all* these tests. Do yours?

CHAPTER 14

PERFORMANCE
MEASUREMENT

YOU UNDERSTAND ALL YOU REALLY NEED TO KNOW ABOUT THE
most important characteristics of investment performance
statistics when you accept as obvious the following proposition:
If many people are in a coin-tossing contest, you can predict two
results with great confidence:

1. In the long, *long* term most coin tossers will average about 50
   percent heads and 50 percent tails.
2. In the *short* to intermediate term, however, some of the coin
   tossers will *appear* to be somewhat better than average at
   tossing heads—or tails—and a very few will appear to be
   much better than average.

If we were to inspect the record, surely the data on each individual coin tosser would be clear and objective. But we'd know
better than to think that the *past* results would be good predictors
of *future* results in coin tossing. Sooner or later each of the coin
tossers would become more and more *average*. As we've seen, stat-
isticians call this powerful yet common phenomenon "regression
to the mean." Understanding the determining power of regression

to the mean is the key to understanding a lot about reported investment performance.

Warning: Performance measurement is least useful when it is needed most—and is needed least when it could be most effective. After careful statistical analysis, quantitative expert Barr Rosenberg estimated that it would require 70 years of observations to show conclusively that even as much as a 2-percent annual incremental return resulted from superior investment management skill rather than chance. This chapter explains why.

Performance data that are sufficiently timely to have relevance for practical decisions on how well a mutual fund is really doing are based on too small a sample or too short a time period to provide enough information to make an accurate objective evaluation. And performance measurement results for longer periods, which offer greater assurance of accuracy, are not sufficiently timely to be relevant for current decisions on how well funds are really doing—unless the results are overwhelmingly good or bad. By the time performance data are good enough for investors to act with confidence, the optimal time for action will be long past.

Measurements of investment performance do not, at least in the short run, "mean what they say." Performance measurement services do not report "results." They report interim statistics. As usually reported in their two-decimal form for a specified time period, investment returns sound almost microscopically accurate: "Over the 12 months ending June 30, manager A returned 27.53 percent." That apparent precision gives such performance numbers an appearance of legitimacy they do not deserve since they are in truth only a sampling—not a measurement—of a long-term series of investment returns. Note that over the long term, no major mutual fund has ever achieved a sustained 2 percent advantage over the market average. However, most of the most advertised funds have achieved at least a 2 percent advantage for the carefully selected period for which performance is being advertised. Caveat emptor.

A form of Gresham's law ("bad money drives out good") can easily take over as fund managers and investors both allow the obsession with short-term performance to drive out thoughtful consideration of longer-term investment practices and objectives. By expressing recent short-term returns in such precise terms, performance measurement turns our heads: It makes us believe that the short term is meaningful and that the long term will resemble it. It almost never does. That's why short-term thinking—Mr. Market's specialty—is the mortal enemy of long-term investment success.

The statistics cited in advertisements are all too often arbitrary short-term samples drawn period by period from a most unusual *continuous* process—the process of managing complex, changing portfolios of securities in the context of a large, dynamic, always changing, and often turbulent free and competitive capital market. The stocks and bonds in the portfolios are frequently changed, companies and their businesses are always changing in many different ways, and the factors that most affect the prices of securities (fear, greed, inflation, politics, economic news, business profits, investors' expectations, and more) never cease to change. So long as your investment portfolio is not being cashed in, this multidimensional set of turbulent change forces will go on and on, revising the value of your portfolio. There are no real "results" until the process stops and the portfolio is liquidated.

Regression to the mean is a central reality of the patterns observed in long time-series of data (such as investment results and coin tossing). The manager whose favorable investment performance in the recent past *appears* to be "proving" that he or she is a better manager is often—not always, but all too often—about to produce *below-average* results. Why? Usually, a large part of the apparently superior performance was *not* due to superior skill that will continue to produce superior results but was instead due to that particular manager's sector of the market temporarily enjoying above-average rates of return—or luck.

When the tide turns, the behavior of the segment of the market that propelled the manager ahead may now hold him or her back. That's one reason that mutual fund managers' results so often regress to the mean. Another reason is this: With so many professional investors being so good at what they do, it is difficult for any one of them to beat the crowd continuously because the crowd is full of well-informed, intensely competitive, and disciplined professionals who play the game very, very well.

Long-term performance data for groups of managers from a fund company or for a style of management will often have both a "survivor bias" and a backdating or "new firm bias." The resulting combined biases can create dangerously deceptive distortions. Survivor bias occurs because new managers are added to the database when their past results are too good to ignore—lifting the composite record higher. And old managers are removed from the data when their results are no longer "acceptable"—again lifting the retroactively revised composite record higher. New firm bias has a related cause: New mutual funds are often "incubated" (to use the industry term), and those with the best recent performance presented to the public as new fund introductions while the others are silently buried as mistakes.

Caveat emptor—again. These two biases can easily add up to 100 basis points per annum. And the distortion produced by these two biases usually equals—and often exceeds—the apparent superiority of selected managers. Advertising will tout the funds with the "best records," so investors will hear most often from those that have been the most successful—so far.

Moreover, as with any series of statistics, the starting point or base year is very important. Many of the most impressive "gee whiz" charts of investment performance become quite ordinary by simply adding or subtracting one or two years at the start or the end of the period shown. Investors should always get the whole record—not just selected excerpts.

For users of performance measurement, a big problem is separating three very different factors that are often mixed together. One factor is the "sampling error"—the probability that the statistics do not precisely equal the reality. As in any sample, there will be imprecision or uncertainty. In investment performance data, the sampling error is the degree to which the particular portfolio, for the particular time period, is or is not a fair and representative sample of the manager's work.

The second factor is that, during the measurement period, the market environment may have been favorable or unfavorable for the particular fund's way of investing. For example, funds of small-capitalization (small-cap) stocks have had both very favorable and very unfavorable market environments during the past few decades. As a result, they have all looked better than they really were in some years and have looked worse than they really were in other periods. This is why investment results should be measured over at *least* one full cycle of up markets and down markets.

The third factor is the skill—or *lack* of skill—of the manager. This is what many clients and managers most want to measure. But here's the rub: In the short run, sampling errors will have a much larger impact on the reported results than will the manager's skill. As noted earlier, it would take many decades of performance measurement to know whether the *apparently* superior results were as a result of the manager's skill or just a result of good luck. By the time you had gathered enough data to determine whether your fund manager really was skillful or just lucky, at least one of you would probably have died of old age.

The power of regression to the mean in investing is illuminated in Figure 14.1. Each column shows—for each quartile—the average annual compound returns achieved by investing with *last*

	Quartile rank in subsequent three years (% persistence)				
Alpha rank: three-year nonoverlapping periods	**First quartile**	**Second quartile**	**Third quartile**	**Fourth quartile**	**Missing**
First quartile	29.2%	16.2%	15.0%	20.6%	19.0%
Second quartile	16.6	24.8	22.3	15.3	21.0
Third quartile	14.7	20.0	22.8	16.0	26.5
Fourth quartile	15.1	14.9	15.3	22.6	32.0

Figure 14.1 Subsequent-year median annual returns for managers, sorted by past year's returns

year's quartile-by-quartile managers for the *next* year. The final column shows the 10-year cumulative average. Even a brief inspection of the annual columns—and particularly the 10-year final column—shows that past performance does not predict future performance.

Most individual investors are aware of the ubiquitous ratings of mutual fund performance coming from Morningstar. But Morningstar's "one-star" to "five-star" ratings report only a fund's past performance. In plain English, the most widely recognized ratings are risky for making investment decisions.

While Morningstar candidly admits that its star ratings have little or no *predictive power*, 100 percent of net new investment money going into mutual funds goes to funds that were recently awarded five stars and four stars. (We've all seen the numerous ads trumpeting the high ratings.) This is too bad because careful research concludes that the ratings are not working: "There is little statistical evidence that Morningstar's highest-rated funds outperform the medium-rated funds."[1] Indeed, in the months after the ratings are handed out each year, the five-star funds generally earn less than half as much as the broad market index! However unintentionally, Morningstar ratings are misleading investors into buying high and selling low. Ugh!

Take a careful look at the data in Figure 14.1. As you'll soon see, there's nothing to see. Net of fees, *there is no pattern*. Like Sherlock Holmes's dog that didn't bark, this lack of pattern *is* the pattern. As Gertrude Stein once said in dismissing the possibility of visiting Oakland, California: "There's no *there* there."

The grievous lack of predictability of future performance on the basis of past performance is shown in Figure 14.2, a stunning comparison of results for the top 20 performers in a *bull* market and the results for the same funds the very next year in a *bear* market.[2]

Rank in bull market*	Rank in bear market*
1	3,784
2	277
3	3,892
4	3,527
5	3,867
6	2,294
7	3,802
8	3,815
9	3,868
10	3,453
11	3,881
12	3,603
13	3,785
14	3,891
15	1,206
16	2,951
17	2,770
18	3,871
19	3,522
20	3,566

*Rank among 3,896 mutual funds in performances during the 12 months ending on March 30, 2000, and the 12 months ending on March 30, 2001.

Figure 14.2 Comparative fund performance in successive bull and bear markets

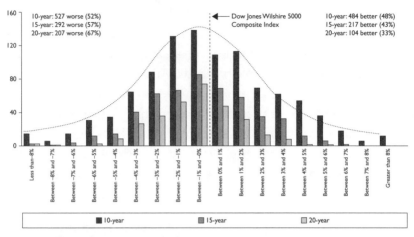

Figure 14.3 After-cost distribution of excess returns of U.S. active equity mutual funds as of December 31, 2006

Over very long periods, the average return obtained by most actively managed mutual funds must be expected to be close to the market average *minus* about 1.5 percent of costs each year for management fees, commissions on transactions, and custody expenses. So even if they are—before costs of operation—slightly ahead of the market, thanks to all their hard work, most fund managers can be expected to lag *behind* the market after fees and expenses (as is explained in Chapter 1 and illustrated in Figure 14.3), and this is what studies of investment performance consistently show (see Figure 14.4).

Proportion of funds	Performance versus market
16%	2% or worse
57	0 to –2%
26	0 to 2%
2	2% or more

Figure 14.4 Long-term performance of mutual funds versus the market

The dominant realities are clear: Over half the mutual funds achieved only market performance or *less* than market performance; only 2 percent of the funds were more than 2 percent ahead of the market over the whole period—and that's before taxes; while a much larger 16 percent were 2 percent or more *worse* than the market. While understandable and even predictable, this record is not encouraging news for investors who want to believe in active investing.

If only 2 percent of mutual funds are significantly "above market" and you share the view that finding the really "right" two in a hundred is not a good game to play with real money, you will also agree that there is one fine alternative: index funds. In addition, as we've seen, income taxes are negligible with index funds because turnover is far lower and the funds can be managed to avoid incurring the tax.

Even more disconcerting for mutual fund investors, the average mutual fund investor ironically gets a return that is significantly *below* the return of the average mutual fund he or she invests in.[3] From 1984 to 1995 the investors' shortfall was a stunning 6 percent annually—investors got only one-half of the 12.3 percent "earned" by the average equity mutual fund. Even investors in *bond* funds got less than their funds did: only 8 percent versus 9 percent. A 1999 study[4] concluded that while the S&P 500 gained an average of 17.9 percent a year over the 15 years from 1984 to 1998, the typical investor in stock funds earned only 7 percent a year over that period. The reason: frequent trading in and out. Instead of staying the course with their mutual funds, many investors tried to time the market, typically holding a fund for less than three years before selling and buying a different fund.

When the income tax consequences of what has become "typical" portfolio turnover—100 percent or more annually—are deducted, mutual fund performance gets cut back even more: typically by as much as 3 percentage points.

Period of time	Percentage fo funds outperforming the market
1 year	35
10 years	25
25 years	10
50 years	5

Figure 14.5 Very few mutual funds outperfom the market over the long term

The odds of outperforming the market get worse and worse—and more significant—as the measurement period gets longer and longer, as shown in Figure 14.5. One study found that only 13.25 percent of surviving mutual funds beat the S&P 500. Note the qualifying term *surviving*. Mutual fund companies bury their mistakes.

A key concept is this: Any unexpected and unexplained deviation from realistic expectation is poor performance. (A sensible proxy for "realistic expectations" of a mutual fund is the average performance of other funds with similar investment objectives.) A large unexplained deviation is very poor performance. And as every user of the statistical techniques of "quality control"[5] knows, it makes no difference whether the deviation is *above* or *below* expectation. Sure, we investors are trained to think that higher returns are better returns, and in the long run they certainly are. But in the shorter run, deviating above or below expectation indicates that the manager is out of conformance with his or her mission. And "out of conformance" usually means out of control—with unhappy results the probable eventual outcome. (A ship is just as far off course when it is 10 miles *west* of its objective as when it is 10 miles *east* of its objective.) It's nice for the investor to get a higher return than a lower return, but either one is off target, and the investor should not confuse good luck (or bad luck) with the manager's level of skill.

A major problem for institutional investment managers and for their clients is the considerable dispersion in the performance being produced by the same investment managers when managing portfolios with the same investment policies. The results should be the same, but the differences can and often are substantial. For an investment manager, such dispersion indicates an important problem in quality control.

Information is data with a purpose. The purpose of measuring performance is to determine whether current portfolio operations are in faithful accord with long-term policy. Because performance measurement can be useful only when a valid standard has been clearly established, the usefulness of performance measurement depends on the clarity and specificity of the investor's investment policy.

One of the great frustrations professional investors have with typical performance measurements is that bad decisions with favorable outcomes are often well received by amateur investors while good decisions with temporarily unfavorable outcomes can lead to a loss of confidence—at just the wrong time. Investors who choose a mutual fund just after it has had its "kind of market" often are imputing to the fund manager a special set of skills and genius that will be impossible to demonstrate after that market environment changes.

The final problem with performance measurement is its perverse tendency to stimulate counterproductive thinking and behavior by diverting your interest and attention to short-term operating results and away from long-term policy. The process of measuring almost certainly influences the phenomenon being measured, as the physicist Werner Heisenberg elucidated years ago with his "principle of indeterminacy."

Sophisticated clients have been able to stay with investment managers who made good qualitative sense even when the quantitative measures of performance were disappointing—particularly when a manager was conscientiously and competently following his or her agreed-upon mandate even though that mandate happened to be temporarily out of tune with the market's favorite sectors. In many cases the subsequent performance has been exceptionally rewarding to both manager and client.

In fact, a good test of the care with which you have chosen a mutual fund would be this: If the fund underperformed the market because the manager's particular style was out of favor, would you cheerfully assign substantially *more* money to that fund? If your answer is yes, you recognize that the manager will almost certainly outperform the overall market averages when investment fashion again favors his or her style. This is the favorable side of regression to the mean, so why not take advantage of the opportunity?

End Notes

1. C. R. Blake and M. R. Money, "Morningstar Ratings and Mutual Fund Performance," *Journal of Financial and Quantitative Analysis*, Vol. 35, No. 3, September 2000.
2. This "now you see it, now you don't" lack of meaning was first and most delightfully shown for individual common stocks years ago by Ian M. D. Little, the investment bursar of Nuffield College at Oxford, in his aptly titled essay "Higgledy, Piggledy, Growth."
3. Gary Belsky and Thomas Gilovich, *Why Smart People Make Big Money Mistakes* (New York, Simon & Schuster, 1999), p. 178.
4. Dalbar, Inc.
5. W. Edwards Deming and Joseph M. Juran built great careers helping manufacturers achieve superior product quality through such statistical techniques for analyzing consistency and conformance to plan and intention.

CHAPTER 15

PREDICTING THE MARKET—ROUGHLY

NVESTORS NATURALLY WANT TO KNOW THE MOST PROBABLE investment outlook for the years ahead. (Understanding the outlook for the next days or weeks is easy. As J. P. Morgan famously said, "It will fluctuate.") Long-term investors understand from experience the remarkable discipline of the bell curve of economic behavior and the central tendency of the major forces in the economy and the stock market to move toward "normal." One good way to be realistic about future returns is to assume that the future range of price/earnings multiples and profits will be within their historical upper and lower limits and will appear with increasing frequency at values closer and closer to the mean.

While the economy is extraordinarily complex at a detailed level—and the stock market reflects all sorts of factors in every domestic and global industry, in thousands of companies, and in the overall economy—two big factors determine the dominant reality for investors: corporate profits (and the dividends they provide) and the price/earnings (P/E) ratio at which these earnings are capitalized. The price/earnings ratio is determined by interest rates—which are driven by expected inflation—plus an "equity premium" reflecting the uncertainty of investing in stocks, plus or minus a "speculative" factor reflecting how optimistic or pessimistic investors currently feel.

Historical perspective is always helpful.[1] How do these two major factors—earnings and P/E—explain America's best-ever bull market in 1982–1999? Here's how: First, corporate profits in 1982 were only 3.5 percent of gross domestic product, significantly *below* the 4 to 6 percent normal range. By the late 1990s corporate profits were almost 6 percent, the *high* side of the normal range. That's a big change. Next, interest rates on long-term U.S. government bonds plunged over that period from 14 percent to 5 percent. (This single change would multiply the market value of those bonds *eight*fold, or 13 percent compounded annually.) As with all long-term changes in the market's valuation, the main forces were fundamental and *objective*. Also included was an additional *subjective* factor that depended on how investors felt: very pessimistic in 1974 and very optimistic in 1999. Over the same years, partly as a result of earnings growth but primarily because of that major decline in interest rates—as expectations for inflation fell substantially—the Dow Jones Industrial Average (with all dividends reinvested) increased nearly *20* times for a compounded annual return of 19 percent.

In cheerful disregard for the great powers driving regression to the mean, investors almost always project the past market and economic behavior into the future, somehow expecting more of the same. In the early 1970s, investors were sure that inflation would stay sky high and earnings would stay low or get even worse, and most newspapers and magazines featured the same grisly prospects. In 2000, investors were remarkably (but almost predictably) highly optimistic, anticipating more of the same compounding—particularly investors who were enamored of Internet stocks and were chanting the mantra of all stock market bubbles: "This time it's different." Other investor enthusiasms were canals in Britain in the 1830s, railroads in Europe and America in the 1850s, automobiles in the 1920s, and real estate in Japan in the 1980s.

By 2007, the dot-com collapse had been forgotten and investors were again comfortable with above-average P/Es. Then the subprime mortgage debacle compounded into a cataclysmic "perfect storm" and slammed the market down as credit markets froze, well-known banks and securities firms were suddenly closed, and fears of a major recession mushroomed. Once again, investors learned how difficult it is to estimate the near-term market more specifically than Mr. Morgan's dictum: "It will fluctuate."

One straightforward approach to estimating the market's longer-term future is to divide investment returns into the *fundamental* return and the *speculative* return. "Fundamental return" is the combination of current dividends and the expected average annual growth in earnings. "Speculative return" is the change— plus *or* minus—in evaluation relative to earnings: the price/earnings ratio. History can tell us a lot.

To start, if dividends yield 1.5 percent and corporate earnings grow at 4.5 percent—the middle of their normal range of growth over the long term—then a composite of 6 percent is the reasonable first part of the "fundamental" rate of return to expect, before adjusting for inflation. Next, what change in valuation, if any, is reasonable? As the starting point, the average price/earnings ratio in recent decades has been about 15.5.

For the period 1901–1921 the inflation-adjusted average annual return of the U.S. stock market was 0.2 percent. For the period 1929–1949 it was 0.4 percent, and for 1966–1986 it was 1.9 percent. In other words, for periods covering more than 60 percent of the twentieth century, the real annual returns generated by the third best performing stock market in the world were less than 2.0 percent. And the first decade of the twenty-first century is almost sure to be worse. At year-end 1964 *and* at year-end 1981, the Dow stood at 875—17 long years with zero net change before adjusting for inflation—because even though corporate profits were up nicely, interest rates had soared from 4 percent to 15 percent, compressing the market's price/earnings multiple substantially, and investors had "learned" to be deeply pessimistic. From that low level, where did the market go?

In 1988, dividends yielded 3.5 percent, and over the next 11 years earnings grew at 7.1 percent annually. Good news for investors: The fundamental return—dividends plus earnings growth—was 10.6 percent per annum. But that's not all: Investors got paid a lot more. While the fundamental return was 10.6 percent, the total investment return was a stunning 18.9 percent. The difference was made up by the add-on of 8.3 percentage points in speculative return as the price/earnings ratio took flight and more than doubled from 12 to 29 at the millennium.

Could it last? Of course not. Regression to the mean was sure to come again. Just as a price/earnings multiple of 12 had been too low—and long-term investors were eventually certain to get a strong lift from mean regression—a price/earnings multiple of 29 was too high and was eventually sure to go down.

Ben Graham wisely cautioned in the introduction to his classic textbook *Security Analysis*[2]: "Long-term investors must be careful not to learn too much from recent experience." He was talking about the 1929 market crash and the ghastly months and years that followed. He could just as easily have been talking about the Internet market or 2008 or any of a long series of times when all or part of the stock market overreacted to recent events—sometimes positively and sometimes negatively—and short-term hopes or fears overwhelmed long-term valuations.

Predicting the stock market *roughly* is not hard, but predicting it accurately is truly impossible. Equally, predicting approximately where the stock market will normally be in the long run is not hard, but even estimating how it will move over the next few months is nearly impossible—and pointless.

End Notes

1. *Irrational Exuberance* (Princeton University Press, 2000), Robert Shiller's eloquent and fact-founded review of the U.S. stock market at the height of the "new economy" euphoria, is a superb example of a rational appraisal.
2. Benjamin Graham, *Security Analysis* (McGraw-Hill, 1934 edition).

CHAPTER 16

THE INDIVIDUAL INVESTOR

INDIVIDUAL INVESTORS ARE PROFOUNDLY DIFFERENT FROM institutional investors like pension funds and endowments. It's not just that individual investors have less money. One difference is decisive: Each individual is mortal. Mortality is a dominant reality for all individual investors—as individuals and as investors—and of course the exact timing of this great reality is not known.

Life *is* short. Those of us who are earning incomes have a finite number of years in which to build our lifetime savings and invest for retirement security. And those who are no longer earning and saving have finite financial resources on which they will depend for the indefinite duration of their lives.

Individual investors' money often takes on great symbolic meaning and can engage investors' emotions powerfully. While the key to success in investing is *rationality*, most investors can't help letting their emotions get involved—and at certain junctures even get the upper hand. Many investors feel that their money represents them and the worth of their lives (as entrepreneurs often identify their value or their self-worth with their companies). This "my money is me" syndrome is particularly common and virulent among elderly people and often causes irascible or even petty behavior. If it happens to someone in your family, be tolerant: It's probably just another way of expressing fear of death.

Yet another important reality is that individual investors have considerable power to affect others—both financially and emotionally—with gifts and bequests made or not made, made larger or smaller than anticipated, or considered fair or unfair. The emotional power and symbolism of money are often more important than its economic power, and individual investors will be wise to deal carefully with both.

All investors share one formidable and all too easily underestimated adversary: inflation. This adversary is particularly dangerous for individual investors—and most particularly dangerous for retired people. Over the long run, inflation is *the* major problem for investors, not the attention-getting daily or cyclical changes in securities prices that most investors fret about. The corrosive power of inflation is truly daunting: At 3 percent inflation—which most people accept as "normal"—the purchasing power of your money is cut in half in 24 years (see Figure 16.1). At 5 percent inflation, the purchasing power of your money is cut in half in less than 15 years—and cut in half *again* in the next 15 years to just one-quarter. For our society where the average person can expect to live to about 85, this is clearly serious

Rate of inflation(%)	Time to cut your money in half (years)
2	24
3	18
4	14
5	12
6	11

Figure 16.1 Effect of increasing inflation on purchasing power

business, particularly when you are retired and have no way to add capital to offset the dreadful erosion of purchasing power caused by inflation.

Individual investors have responsibilities they take very personally: educating children, providing security for themselves—particularly in retirement—and their loved ones, helping to pay for health care for elderly relatives, contributing to the schools and other institutions from which they have benefited or hope their communities will benefit, and more. In addition, individual investors want to provide a strong self-defense against catastrophe, including the risk of living longer and needing more health care than anticipated. Finally, most individuals wish to leave something to their children or grandchildren to enhance *their* lives. Children having better lives than their parents and grand parents is, for most people, the real meaning of progress. Not only are these responsibilities taken personally, but for some needs—particularly health care late in life—the amount of money that will be required is unknown and may become almost unlimited.

Most individual investors have a long-term implicit "balance sheet" of assets and responsibilities, but most have not examined their total financial picture or put it all down on paper. And most have not been explicit about the direct and indirect stakeholders—the "we"—in their balance sheet responsibilities. Doing so would be useful and informative.

In planning the responsibility side of your investor's balance sheet, you'll want to decide who is included in your "we" and for what purpose. How much responsibility do you plan to take for your children's education? College is costly. Graduate school is increasingly accepted as the norm, and it's costly too. After providing for education, is helping with a child's first home important to you? Help in starting a business or a dental practice? How about your parents, brothers and sisters, or your in-laws? Under what circumstances would they need your financial help? How much might be involved and when? Be sure you know what your total commitments might add up to and when the money might be needed.

Because we can invest only what we have saved, saving necessarily comes before investing. Saving has one special characteristic: You can decide what you want done, and you can *make* it happen! Buying straw hats in the fall or Christmas cards in January and saving through the many other daily forms of conscientious "underspending" can make a splendid difference over the years, particularly when it is matched with a sensible long-term approach to investing. One powerful way to save is to limit your spending to *last* year's income.

The first purpose of saving is to accumulate a "defensive reserve" that, like a fire extinguisher, can be turned to for help if and when trouble comes. And like a fire extinguisher, such a reserve should be used boldly and fully whenever needed. If you use your defensive reserve cautiously or only partially, you will simply require a proportionately larger reserve—and it's expensive in opportunity costs to have a larger reserve than is really needed. The reserve is on hand to be *spent*, not to be held back in time of need. After providing for protection against serious contingencies, your further savings can be invested for the long term.

One of the core concepts and basic themes of this book is that funds available for long-term investment will do best for the investor if they are invested in stocks and *kept* in stocks over the long term. But what about elderly investors whose life expectancy is less than the 10 years that approximates "long term"? Shouldn't they, as the conventional wisdom would have it, invest primarily in bonds to preserve capital? As usual, the conventional wisdom may be wrong.

While retired investors may decide for peace of mind that they prefer to invest in relatively stable securities with relatively high income, they may be letting their emotional interests dominate their economic interests. Investing in bonds to generate more current income incurs this economic penalty: Over time, $1 of extra income costs about $1.50 in the total return forgone by not investing as much in long-term equity investments. This can be a heavy price to pay for the apparent conservatism of shifting assets into higher-yielding "defensive" investments such as bonds and income stocks—and becoming a stationary target for inflation to do its corrosive harm.

While an elderly investor may not expect to live for many years, her investments, after being inherited by her beneficiaries, may have a very long-term mission. There may be no reason to limit the time horizon for thinking about investments to the owner's lifetime when the owner's true objectives—providing for children, spouse, or alma mater—have a much longer-term horizon. Besides, one of the secrets to a long and happy life is to "keep climbing" and stay, in Disraeli's felicitous phrase, "in league with the future." Investing in stocks helps keep us young.

To be a truly successful lifetime investor, the first and central challenge is to know thyself—understand your personal financial goals and what would truly be successful for *you*. Remember "Adam Smith's" wise counsel: "If you don't know who you are, the stock market is an expensive place to find out." So are the markets for real estate, commodities, and options.

Investors will be wise to take time to learn as much as possible about themselves—and how they will feel and behave as investors. We need to know our true selves so we can put our best rational thinking in control of our own emotions. For example, here's a simple test—with a friendly twist.

Question: If you had your choice, which would you prefer?
Choice A: Stocks go *up*—by quite a lot—and *stay up* for several years.
Choice B: Stocks go *down*—by quite a lot—and *stay down* for several years.

Make your choice *before* you look at the next page.

Without looking ahead, which did you choose? If you selected choice A, you would be joining 90 percent of the investors—individual and professional—who've taken this test. Comforted to know that most pros are with you? You shouldn't be. Unless you are a long-term *seller* of stocks, you would have chosen *against* your own interests if you chose A.

Here's why. First, remember that when you buy a common stock, what you really buy is the right to receive the dividends paid on that share of stock.[1] Just as we buy cows for their milk and hens for their eggs, we buy stocks for their current and future earnings and dividends. If you ran a dairy, wouldn't you prefer to have cow prices low when you were buying so that you could get more gallons of milk for your investment in cows?

The lower the price of the shares when you buy, the more shares you will get for every $1,000 you invest and the greater the amount of dollars you will receive in future dividends on your investment. Therefore, if you are a saver and a buyer of shares— as most investors are and will continue to be for many years— your real long-term interest is, curiously, to have stock prices go *down* quite a lot and stay there so you can accumulate more shares at lower prices and therefore receive more dividends with the savings you invest.

Thus, the right long-term choice is the counterintuitive choice B. This can be the key insight that may enable you to enjoy greater success as an investor *and* greater peace of mind during your investing career. You may even learn to see a benefit in bear markets. If you're really rational, you will.

Most investors, being all too human, much prefer stock markets that have been rising and feel most enthusiastic about buying more shares when stock prices are already high, axiomatically causing the future rate of return from their dividends to be low. (The dollars of dividends to be received will be the same per share of stock whether you pay a lot or a little for the shares.) Similarly, most investors feel quite negative about stocks *after* share prices have gone down and are most tempted to sell out at the really wrong time—when prices are already low *and* the future dividend yield on the price paid will be high (see Figure 16.2).

If you can use the insight from our simple price quiz and incorporate the rational answer into your investment thinking and behavior, you will appreciate that your emotions often move contrary to your rational economic interests. You will school yourself to go against the crowd and your own feelings,

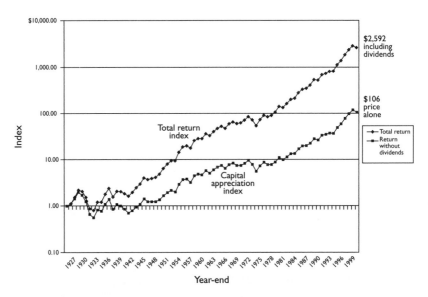

Figure 16.2 This chart shows how important reinvesting dividends has been, even over two long periods when stocks achieved virtually no appreciation: the 25 years from 1930 to 1955 and the 20 years from 1965 to 1985. As shown in the chart, $1.00 grew to $105.96 as a result of price appreciation, with no dividends reinvested, but that $1.00 grew to become $2,591.79 with dividends reinvested.

and will strive to avoid the temptation to jump on the bandwagon to buy when stocks are high or jump off when stocks are low.

Don't confuse facts with feelings. Strive to be consistently rational, and don't focus on the day-to-day and even hour-to-hour ups and downs of stock prices. Rationally, we know that most of the changes in share prices are just "noise," almost random fluctuations. Investors should ignore the dance of stock prices, fascinating and seductive as the activity of Mr. Market may be.

In my first year on Wall Street I was in a training program with a group of freshly minted MBAs. We all looked forward to our final session: a meeting with the senior partner, a patrician who had amassed a fortune through astute investing over many years.[2] Asked about his secret for success and what he would advise young men like us to do, he took a long, thoughtful pause and then summarized his accumulated experience in this blunt maxim: "Don't lose!"

When I first heard his advice nearly 50 years ago, it seemed simplistic, but as the years have gone by, I've become convinced that the advice was and is very sound. Don't set yourself up for serious, irrevocable losses. Naturally, you can't invest without absorbing lots of small interim losses because markets do fluctuate, but don't take untoward risks. Don't swing for the fences. Don't invest with borrowed money. As mentioned earlier, there are no old, bold pilots.

If you find yourself getting caught up in the excitement of a rising market or distressed by a falling market, stop. Break it off. Go for a walk and cool down. Otherwise, you will soon become part of the "crowd," wanting to *do* something—and you will start making mistakes, perhaps grave mistakes that you will later regret. Benign neglect is, for most investors, the secret to long-term success in investing.

You can increase your chances of achieving superior investment performance—which means reliably achieving your own explicit and realistic investment objectives—by taking the time once a year for a formal review of your investment objectives, financial resources, financial responsibilities, and recent investment results compared with prior realistic expectations. This is the time—and yearly is the right interval—to rebalance to your intended asset mix. Keep written records of your reviews; you'll learn a lot about yourself and your capabilities by reviewing past reviews.

Although the focus of your attention typically will be on investments, the following should also be examined: savings, insurance, bank credit available, current debts, probable obligations to help or support others in your "we" group, annual income versus expenditures, and estate plans. The objective of this disciplined exercise is to "turn on the lights" and look over your whole situation.

If you have successfully saved and invested enough to have ample funds for all your chosen responsibilities or obligations, you have truly *won* the money game. Bravo! This is an appropriately thrilling achievement.

Winners should be careful never to put their victory back at risk, particularly through unnecessarily borrowing or committing too much to any single investment or overextending responsibilities and commitments.

Winners should avoid speculating in an attempt to win *big*. It's not worth the risk of becoming a big loser—truly a sucker. Winners should also be careful about being too careful. A shift to nominally "conservative" investing can leave investments exposed—and at risk—to the erosion of inflation. Nathan Mayer Rothschild, the founder of that family's great fortune, explained what it takes: "It requires a great deal of boldness and a great deal of caution to make a great fortune; and when you have got it, it requires ten times as much wit to keep it."

As an individual investor, these 10 "commandments" may be useful guides to thinking about your decisions on investments:

1. Save. Invest your savings in your future happiness and security and education for your kids.
2. Don't speculate. If you must "play the market" to satisfy an emotional itch, recognize that you are gambling on your ability to beat the pros so limit the amounts you play with to the same amounts you would gamble with the pros at Las Vegas. (Keep accurate records of your results, and you'll soon persuade yourself to quit!)
3. Don't do anything in investing primarily for tax reasons. Tax shelters are poor investments. Tax loss selling is primarily a way for brokers to increase their commissions. There are exceptions: Be sure you have an astute estate plan that is current with your financial situation and the ever-changing tax laws. Making charitable gifts of low-cost stock that has appreciated in value can make sense *if* you were going to sell the stock anyway. Set up an IRA if you can, and maximize contributions to your tax-sheltered 401(k) or profit-sharing plan every year. If you have investments outside your 401(k), make your investment decisions based on the total picture: To minimize income taxes, any bonds or bond funds belong in your tax-sheltered retirement fund.
4. Don't think of your home as an investment. Think of it as a place to live with your family—period. All too many families learned this lesson in the recent past as

(Continued)

the historically unusual price run-up in house prices
got suddenly and forcefully reversed in 2008.

A home is not a good financial investment and
never was. But a home can certainly be a fine
investment in your family's happiness. Over the
30 years to year-end 2007—before the nationwide
decline—the value of an average home rose at
5.5 percent a year. Of this, 4.1 percent was just
inflation. Costs—taxes, insurance, and routine
maintenance—were 3 percent. So a home was not a
good investment even before house prices dropped
sharply in 2008.

5. Don't do commodities. Consider the experience of a
commodities broker who over a decade advised
nearly 1,000 customers on commodities. How many
made money? Not even one.[3] But the broker did,
thanks to commissions. Oh sure, many commodities
have had huge prices run-ups in the early years of
this century—and rundowns in 2008. Dealing in
commodities is really only price speculation. It's not
investing because there's no economic productivity
or value added.

6. Don't get confused about stockbrokers and mutual
fund salespeople. They are usually very nice people,
but their job is not to make money *for* you. Their job
is to make money *from* you. While a few stockbrokers
are wonderfully conscientious people who are
devoted to doing a good, thoughtful job for the
customers they work with over many, many years,
you can't *assume* that your stockbroker is working
that way for you. Some do, but most simply can't

(Continued)

afford it. Be realistic. The typical stockbroker "talks to" 200 customers with *total* invested assets of $5 million. To earn $100,000 a year, he or she needs to generate about $300,000 in gross commissions, or 6 percent of the money she talks to. To generate this volume of commissions—heavy expenses to the investors—the broker cannot afford the time to learn what is "right." He or she has to keep the money moving—and it will be *your* money.

7. Don't invest in new or "interesting" investments. They are all too often designed to be *sold to* investors, not to be *owned by* investors. (When the novice fisherman expressed wonderment that fish would actually go for the gaudily decorated lures offered at the bait shop, the proprietor's laconic reply was, "We don't sell them lures to fish.")

8. Don't invest in bonds just because you've heard that bonds are conservative or for safety of either income or capital. Bond prices can fluctuate nearly as much as stock prices do, and bonds are a poor defense against the major risk of long-term investing—inflation.

9. Write out your long-term goals, your long-term investing program, and your estate plan—and stay with them. While annual reviews are recommended, review these plans at least once each decade.

10. Distrust your feelings. When you feel euphoric, you're probably in for a bruising. When you feel down, remember that it's darkest just before dawn, so take no action. Activity in investing is almost always in surplus supply. Less *is* better.

Finally, here is a special word to those who participate in a 401(k) plan—or any other "defined contribution" plan—over which you, as a participant, have investment discretion. Concentrate on index funds. Do not invest in your own company—wonderful as the company may be—because depending on your job at one company is already a major concentration of your "total economic portfolio." Your retirement fund should be for safety first, and safety means *defense*. If you have any doubts, read all about Polaroid and Enron—two of numerous major U.S. companies that later lost all their market value and were forced to lay off large numbers of loyal workers, resulting in retirement savings lost, jobs lost, and dreams lost.

If you're still inclined to believe you or anyone else can profitably select active investment managers, please look at the record. It's not encouraging. For example, if you really believe you can and will pick active investment managers who will outperform the market average and index funds, please consider these facts:

- Over 10-year periods, three out of four active managers' results fall below the market averages—and below index funds. Over longer periods, more fall below.
- Those managers who fall short fall short by more than those who do better do better.
- Pension executives and investment consultants who specialize in selecting the best managers have, as a group, been unsuccessful at selecting managers who can beat the market. If these hardworking, conservative professional "buyers" are not, on average, able to succeed, why should you and I believe we can?

You've already learned that past performance records do not predict future results. In fact, if you divide all managers into deciles by their past results, the data have zero predictive power—with this one exception: The worst losers do tend to keep losing.

If you do decide to select active investment managers, promise yourself you will stay with your chosen manager for many years—at least a decade—because the data show that changing managers is not only expensive, but it usually doesn't work. While we all know we could, in theory, do very well by getting out of a fund before it has a bad run and into another fund just before it has a great run, that just does not happen. Actually, reality is closer to the opposite. On average, individuals pour money into funds *after* they've had their best run and move out after the worst period. That's why mutual funds actually perform better than the investors in those same funds.

End Notes

1. Yes, you also get the right to vote on the selection of auditors, the election of directors, and so forth. And you get the right to be bought out at a higher price if and when there's a future takeover. But realistically, few votes of shareholders go against management's recommendations, and unanticipated buyouts occur at few companies, so these shareholder rights are usually not very important compared with dividends. Yes, you also get the right to sell the stock to another investor, hopefully at a higher price. But what determines the price the next investor will gladly pay? The present value of expected future earnings and dividends.
2. Joseph K. Klingenstein of Wertheim & Co.
3. John Train, *The Money Masters* (New York: Harper & Row, 1987).

CHAPTER 17

SELECTING FUNDS

IF YOU ARE UNABLE OR UNWILLING TO ACCEPT INDEXING—yet—you have two alternatives: You can make your own investment decisions, or you can invest in actively managed mutual funds. If, after reading this short book, you still decide to pick your own stocks, do yourself a favor and keep a careful record of your decisions, what you expected when you made them, and how they worked out.

Stockbrokers may say that you pay nothing for their investment advice, their firm's research, or all the services you get. But take time to study the whole picture, and you'll soon find that the stockbrokerage commissions you'll be paying can easily add up over a year's time to a much higher total cost as a percent of your assets then a mutual fund.

Investing is *not* a hobby. Every major study has found that average results for self-reliant individual investors are poor. Moreover, the dispersion of results above and below that average is quite wide, so all too many investors get stuck with *very* poor results. That's why stockbrokers typically lose more than 20 percent of their customers every year. And the customers lose real money that the stockbroker can never win back.

You may still want to select your own mutual fund, so here's a suggestion. You can jump-start your search by getting a list of the leaders in 401(k)s or other defined contribution plans from *Money, Forbes,* or *BusinessWeek* and then asking your most knowledgeable acquaintances which of these funds consistently attract the best people and are most likely to achieve good results over the very long term. Your list will soon be dominated by such outstanding organizations as American Funds (managed by Capital Group Companies), T. Rowe Price, and Vanguard.[1]

When selecting an actively managed mutual fund, make your selection in a deliberately unorthodox way. Do *not* pick one fund. Instead start with a "ballpark" decision. Rather than trying to find *the* best mutual fund, look for a superior investment organization that offers a full "family" of mutual funds. The key to long-term success is not found in the last few years' performance numbers; it's in the professional culture of the organization. Stocks and investment ideas come and go; fund managers come and go; but character in a person and culture in an organization—good or bad—are hard to change. So look for the culture that attracts and keeps superior people for 30- or 40-year careers. Look for consistency in statements about "how we do things here." And be wary and skeptical about organizations that try to get you to focus on recent results when your interests are all long term. Eventually, character or organizational culture will surely dominate.

This means that you're looking for a well-established organization with a good long-term record that is respected and admired by knowledgeable investment people and will be *comfortable to live with.* Ask around: Is that organization considered a great place to work that consistently attracts and keeps first-rate people and manages itself primarily as a *professional* organization rather than a *commercial* organization?

The idea of "comfortable to live with" is the key to long-term investment success for most individuals investing in mutual funds. "Change" is the investor's enemy in two ways. First, the cost of changing mutual funds may *look* small—switching funds "only costs a few percent" of assets—if done rarely, but all too many of those who change funds do so every few years, and those costs of change keep adding up. Second, most investors who change funds pay much larger, but hidden, costs because they sell after the worst part of the losses and buy after the best part of the gains. Watch the total industry money flows. Most of the selling comes after a fund has already underperformed, and most of the buying comes after a fund has already outperformed. And the inflows and outflows are largest for the funds with the most dramatic ups and downs—so the self-inflicted pain is all the worse.

Some mutual fund organizations are skilled at the business of selling or "asset gathering," but are not focused on the *professional* disciplines of successful investing. They are dangerous to investors and, eventually, to themselves—like politicians who know how to get elected but not how to govern or the dog that, after running and running, actually catches the car and doesn't know what to do with it.

Sales-driven mutual fund companies look back with understandable pride at how very far they've come as entrepreneurial businesses. But all too few recognize that in winning the confidence of 100 million individuals and over half of the families in the United States, mutual fund companies have not only won the battle for business success; they have also transformed themselves from business organizations into fiduciary organizations. Years ago, mutual funds were small *private* businesses; they are *public* now whether they recognize it or not—because they have accepted the public trust. The standards are very different now. The industry's "winners" had better get used to it and refocus their priorities away from sales to good stewardship or they will lose the trust of millions of individual investors—and become unintended losers of business themselves.

How many different mutual funds should you use? With mutual funds, an investor usually can find several different styles or classes of investing offered by any one major family of funds: index funds of different kinds, growth funds versus value funds, large cap versus small cap, money markets, REITs (real estate investment trusts), international versus global, and many more. All the funds offered by a well-managed family of funds will be organizationally accountable for the same standards of professionalism, reasonable fees, and investor service. That's why it makes sense to concentrate your mutual fund investing with one fund family whose long-term investment results and business values and practices you respect.

Start by knowing what your own investment objectives and staying power really are. Determining your tolerance for pain and investment staying power will provide you with the basis for which you can set the level of market risk that you can and will live with. Don't overcommit. Know your internal realities and stay within your own limitations. As my father wisely advised: "Never risk more than you know you can afford to lose."[2]

Study your own record of decisions over the years to see how well *you* perform as an investor, and examine your capacity to tolerate market adversity in different time frames. It's one thing to know your ability to handle quarter-to-quarter fluctuations: They are usually relatively modest and soon reversed.

It's another thing to absorb and accept a full bear market, particularly one that lasts longer and plummets more than normal. For example, ask: How did you feel when stocks lost over 45 percent of their value in 2008? How did you feel—and how did you act—under the ferocious pressures as day after day the market surged up and down, mostly down, as the Fed and Treasury and central banks around the world rushed to save the financial system, and leading organizations either failed (Lehman Brothers, Bear Stearns,

Wachovia, and Washington Mutual) or teetered on the brink (AIG, Merrill Lynch, Citigroup, and Morgan Stanley)?

Next, learn to understand the *external* realities of the investment markets and do not expect more of your managers than they can deliver. If you insist on "beat the market" performance, you *will* find mutual fund salespeople who will make that promise. But will they—can they—really keep that promise? Most will not—and identifying in advance the few who will is not easy.

Then—if you still prefer active management over indexing—select mutual funds that have managers who are clearly competent to complete the mission you have in mind. A good rule that is simple to state but very difficult for most investors to follow is this: Never choose a mutual fund you would not confidently "double up" if the fund's performance was significantly behind the market for two or three years and popular opinion was that the fund's manager had lost his or her touch.

Finally, strive to discipline yourself to keep faith with your own commitment to a steady, long-term program. Ignore Mr. Market's shenanigans. When Mr. Market misbehaves, follow the advice of Caesar: *De minimus non curat praetor!* (Don't be concerned with small matters!)

Never terminate a mutual fund solely for below-market performance over a one- or two-year period. You know from personal experience at ticket counters and airport security lines that it does not pay to switch from one line to another. Switching investment managers is even less productive—and switching funds is costly. Staying with a competent mutual fund manager who is conforming to his or her own promises—particularly when he or she is out of phase with the current market environment—shows real "client prudence" in investing and ultimately will be rewarded.

Wise investors choose mutual funds carefully and then stay the course. Very wise and very well-informed investors go one step further: Having selected a small group of long-term "finalists"—chosen because their internal cultures ensure striving for professional excellence over the long term—they pick the mutual fund whose recent results were most depressed by an adverse market environment. They can often get an extra lift from a subsequently more favorable market environment by riding the regression to the mean.

Since you start with an easy answer—using index funds—be sure the decision to pay up for an actively managed fund is the right decision for you. Selecting superior mutual funds for the future is *hard*. As we've seen, most of the investment consulting firms that have specialized for years in selecting investment managers—and have large research staffs poring over all the managers' records and asking them all sorts of questions—are typically *not* successful. The managers the experts select after all their care and diligence do not, on average, outperform the market averages. Cambridge Associates reports candidly, "There is no sound basis for hiring or firing managers solely on the basis of recent performance."

If you decide you are going to select actively managed mutual funds, be sure you recognize the gauntlet you will be running and the difficult decisions you'll need to make correctly:

- Which fund families, if any, will outperform the market for many years into the future?
- Can you identify the future's favored few today?
- Will you make the right decisions and take the right action at the right time?
- If you do select a superior fund, will that fund stay superior, or will the assets managed grow so much, the fund manager's organization change so much, or the fund manager's personal "life situation" change so much that the manager will no longer produce those superior results?

- If the fund's investment performance appears disappointing, will you be able to tell whether it's just temporary and will soon be reversed or whether it is actually the first in a series of future disappointments? If, however reluctantly, you resolve to terminate this fund, you'll have to move on to the next section of the gauntlet and face the same difficult decisions all over again.

Changing mutual funds is especially expensive if your funds have a "load" or sales charge. Even if there's no sales charge, there's that evidence that shows that most investors are late to leave and late—often very late—on getting into the next fund. And watch out: Those oh so caring and helpful salespeople make their money by convincing you to *change* funds. Friendly as they may be, they may be no friend to your long-term investment success.

There is another kind of cost: If you accept the idea that changing funds is really just a normal part of life, chances are you'll select funds less carefully. In that case you'll be part of the problem, not part of the solution, and you will need to keep changing funds that were not chosen with sufficient care. "Dating" mutual funds is a self-destructive cycle; don't get caught up in it.

Many mutual fund managers—particularly those managing large funds—act as though their real goal is to maximize the probability of keeping the assets they have already accumulated. This could and does result in most funds "hugging the index" or "closet indexing" with, typically, 80 percent—or more—of their portfolio. This leaves only 20 percent of the portfolio trying to justify 100 percent of the fees. That's not very likely.

Rare is the mutual fund that achieves long-term results substantially superior *after* adjustment for risk. The data are as grim as a photograph of the 1913 graduating class of St. Cyr—France's military academy—destined for combat in the trenches of World

War I. For over 50 years, mutual funds in the aggregate lost 180 basis points compounded annually to the S&P 500, returning 11.8 percent versus 13.6 percent for the benchmark index.[3] Over the past decade, index funds' returns have been better than the results of more than 80 percent of all U.S. mutual funds. After years of careful study, Princeton's popular professor Burt Malkiel has found that the best estimate of a mutual fund's future performance relative to other mutual funds is based on just two factors: portfolio turnover and expenses. (In both cases, less is more.)

Finally, here are some points to consider on fees. Fees for investment management are much, much more important than they appear to be to most investors. Fees have been going up—substantially—over the years even though the results of a majority of mutual funds do not keep up with the market averages. Conventionally, management fees are presented as a percentage of assets and are seen as "only" around 1 percent of assets.

But wait. Ask yourself: Should clients consider fees as a percentage of assets *or* as a percentage of returns—or, even better, as a percentage of incremental returns achieved over and above the market risk-adjusted return? When thinking about costs, be sure to frame your questions correctly—in proportion to incremental income, not assets. Let's take a look.

If a fund manager says the fee is "only 1 percent," he or she means 1 percent of assets. But if you get an average annual rate of return as high as 9 percent, you might say that the manager's fee is closer to 10 percent. Look still closer, please. You already own all the assets, and you can get 9 percent by investing in low-cost index funds. So the fund manager can only help you by providing *incremental* returns—after adjusting for risk. Can he or she really increase your returns by 200 basis points? If so, *you* will be taking all the risk, and the manager's real fee will be 50 percent— 50 percent of real value added. If returns are increased by only 100 basis points, the real fee will be 100 percent, and you're still putting up all the money and taking all the risks. And if the manager does not add that much value—and most don't because they can't—your fees are on their way toward infinity.

If you think that the level of fees should be in proportion to the actual benefit the fund shareholder gets, you'll be impressed to learn that the fees most mutual funds charge—relative to incremental risk-adjusted returns—are *over* 100 percent. That's right: *All* the value added—plus some—goes to the manager, and there's nothing left over for the investors who put up all the money and took all the risk. It *is* a funny business—and worth thinking about.

End Notes

1. Full disclosure: I've written a book celebrating Capital Group and, years ago, chose to be and still am a director of Vanguard, and I consulted on strategy for many years with T. Rowe Price.

2. In the mid-1970s I increased my commitment to John Neff's Gemini Fund—not by more than I could afford to lose, but by a lot. I knew John well enough to know that he was careful to control and limit risk. Conventional investors were not discriminating carefully between real risk and perception, but John clearly would. The stock market had been negative on the "value" stocks John liked to own. As a closed-end duofund—with one class of shares getting all the dividend income and a second class getting all the capital gains—Gemini's Capital shares had experienced the leveraged impact of a several-year decline in the value area of the stock market *and* were selling at a discount from net asset value. I calculated how much broker's margin could be used without getting a margin call—even after a 20 percent further drop in stock prices—and bought in, fully margined. As the market rose,

I enjoyed the "six-layered" benefits: John Neff as my investment manager, plus the recovery of the market, plus the superior returns to "value" stocks, plus the shift from "discount" to "premium" in the Gemini Capital shares, plus the leverage of the duo-fund, plus the leverage of heavy margin. Despite all the apparent leverage risk, I felt very confident—and quite safe—because I knew that John was both rigorously risk-averse and a disciplined, rational investor. The following 20 years, thanks to John's great work as the professional investor's favorite investment professional, were very well rewarded—with minimal risk.

3. John C. Bogle, "The Clash of Cultures in Investing: Complexity versus Simplicity," speech given at the Money Show, Orlando, Florida, February 3, 1999.

CHAPTER 18

PLANNING YOUR PLAY

YES, DEATH *IS* EVERY INDIVIDUAL'S ULTIMATE REALITY, BUT AS an *investor*, you may well be making too much of it. If, for example, you plan to leave most of your capital in bequests to your children, the appropriate "time horizon" for your family investment policy—even if you are well into your seventies or eighties—may be so long term that you'd be correct to ignore investment conventions such as "older people should invest in bonds for higher income and greater safety "or "to determine the percentage of your assets you should have in stocks, subtract your age from 100."

The wiser, better decision for you and your family might be to invest 100 percent in equities because your "investing horizon" is far longer than your "living horizon." If the people you love (your family and heirs) or even the organizations you love (your favorite charities) are likely to outlive you—as they almost certainly will—perhaps you should extend your "investment planning horizon" to cover not just your own life span but theirs as well. If, for instance, you are 40 years old and have a 5-year-old son, your real investment horizon may not be just another 45 years (your own future life expectancy), but closer to the 80 more years your son will live—particularly for any funds you plan to leave to him. Even if you are 75 years old, your investment horizon could be equally long if you have young grandchildren or a favorite charity.

We investors are mortal, but our investments don't know it—and frankly don't care. Remember another of "Adam Smith's" admonition: "The stock doesn't know you own it." This observation applies to all investments: stocks, bonds, buildings, and so forth. All have value today and will have a future value irrespective of who owns them. Therefore, investing should be done for investment reasons, not for such personal reasons as your age.

So don't change your investments just because you have reached a certain age or have retired. If you could afford fine paintings, you wouldn't change the ones you love the most simply because you reached retirement or celebrated your seventieth or eightieth birthday. It's the same with investments: Why not maintain the long-term strategy you have designed for yourself?

Compounding *is* powerful. Remember the grateful sultan who offered to reward his vizier generously for a great deed that had saved the sultan's empire. The vizier modestly offered to accept only one grain of wheat on the first square of a checkerboard, only two grains on the next, four grains on the third, eight grains on the fourth, and so on and on and on. The crafty vizier said he had no need for a great reward and that the symbolism of this compounding giving would please his humble, grateful heart. Joyfully, the sultan seized upon this seemingly simple way to clear his obligation, but he did not reckon on the formidable power of compounding. Anything doubled 64 consecutive times will balloon—and balloon again. In the story, the few grains of wheat compounded to a total value that was greater than all the wealth in the empire. To defend his honor before Allah, the sultan ended up turning over the entire empire to the vizier.

All investors need to understand the impact on them and their investments coming from two kinds of risks: "market risk" and "inflation risk." Figure 18.1 shows how these two unavoidable

	Nominal returns			Real returns		
1926–2006 total returns	Average annual return	Percent of years with negative return	Highest annual loss	Average annual return	Percent of years with negative return	Highest annual loss
100% T-bills	3.8%	0%	0.0%	0.8%	35%	−15.0%
100% bonds	5.2	9%	−2.3	2.1	38	−14.5
100% stocks	10.5	30	−43.1	7.2	35	−37.3

Source: Adapted from Vanguard Investment Counseling & Research

Figure 18.1 Trade-off between market risk and inflation risk

risks trade off over 80 years. The first three columns show nominal returns with stocks producing nearly three *times* the returns to Treasury Bills—and T-bills never show a loss. The second three columns—adjusted for inflation—tell a very different story. The real return on stocks are a full nine times the returns on T-Bills.

And note the percent of years with negative returns. Before adjusting for inflation, T-Bills never lose and stocks are negative 30 percent of the time, But *after* adjusting for inflation, T-Bills and stocks *both* have negative returns 35 percent of the time. (Bonds are slightly worse).

The message is not how wonderfully compounding increases real wealth. The message has two parts: The second part is that inflation relentlessly destroys wealth's purchasing power almost as rapidly as economic gains build wealth. Only the real net gain is spendable.

Beware of the promotional materials and advertising that are deceiving investors with a Lorelei promise of phenomenal riches in the future without explaining the grimly negative—and simultaneous—impact of inflation as the ruthless, unrelenting destroyer of your capital. To purchase an item costing $100 in 1960 would have cost over $700 in 2008.

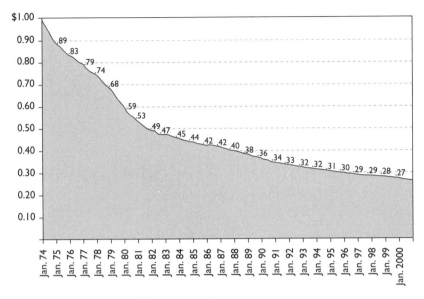

Source: *Consumer Price Index, U.S. Department of Labor*

Figure 18.2 The shrinking value of the dollar.

The corrosive power of inflation is the investor's worst enemy. In just 20 years, as shown in Figure 18.2, the purchasing power of $1 shrank to 35 cents. The power of inflation to impose real harm on investments may be seen by studying the Dow Jones Industrial Average *after* adjustment for inflation. Note particularly:

• From 1977 to 1982, the inflation-adjusted Dow Jones Industrial Average took a five-year loss of 63 percent.

• Rational, long-term investors should know and remember that in the 15 years from the late 1960s to the early 1980s the unweighted stock market, adjusted for inflation, plunged by about 80 percent. As a result, the decade of the 1970s was actually worse for investors than the decade of the 1930s.

- In 1993, the Dow Jones Industrial Average was equal to its inflation-adjusted level at the peak of a highly speculative "bubble" market in 1929. Even when comparing a far overpriced base and ignoring all the dividends received over all those years, 65 years was a long, long time to wait to get even.

In developing a sound financial plan, investors will want to begin with good answers ("good" because they are both comforting and rational) to these three overarching questions:

- Does my plan assure me of having enough income to pay for an appropriate standard of living after overcoming inflation during retirement? For most people, this "sufficiency of income" works out to 75 to 80 percent of preretirement spending plus 3 to 4 percent compounded annually to offset inflation.
- Will our financial reserves be sufficient to cover unexpected emergencies—usually health crises—particularly in old age? Beware! Eighty percent of a typical person's lifetime expenditures on health care are spent in the last six months of life. Women live longer than men, and wives are often younger than their husbands. Therefore, most couples will want to pay particular attention to providing adequately for the wife's years as a widow.
- Will the remaining capital match our goals and intentions for giving to heirs and charities?

If these core questions are not answered fully and affirmatively, your plan needs to be reconsidered and changed, perhaps substantially. If change is called for, do it now so that you'll have time on your side, working for you as long as possible. Write down your goals—with the target dates by which you intend to achieve them—so you can measure your actual progress compared to your explicit plan, because in all matters of investing time is key.

Investment decisions are not necessarily best when driven by noninvestment events such as the timing of children's admission to college, the receipt of an inheritance, and the date of retirement, so separate *when* you invest from *how* you invest. Your investments do not know your wishes or intentions—and really don't care. As an investor, you must adapt to the market. The market won't adapt to you.

Over your lifetime as an investor, your optimal investment program will change—and change again—partly because your circumstances and resources will change and partly because your objectives and priorities will change. But the more thoughtfully and soundly you plan and the further in advance you do your planning, the less you will need to change your plan as time passes. Planning a sound long-term investment program is often done best in 10-year chunks of time. This helps because working with decades reminds us that sound investing is inherently long term in nature.

Of course, planning is only as useful as the actual implementation that follows. You will want to follow the wise coach's twin admonitions: "Plan your play, and play your plan."

The first step is clear: Get out of debt. It's a well-earned great feeling when you achieve the first victory of paying off your school loans and the debts you incurred while you were setting up your first household. The key to getting out of debt is clear—save!

A lifetime based on the habit of thrift—spending less than you might and deferring the spending you do—is essential to saving. Those who assume or hope that their incomes will somehow outstrip their spending may believe in magic, but they are doomed to be disappointed, often grievously. "Pay yourself first" by putting money into savings on a regular basis. A dollar-cost-averaging account with a mutual fund, which automatically deducts a fixed dollar amount each month from your bank account or paycheck, is a good way to pay yourself first. And if your employer has a defined-contribution retirement plan, be sure you participate at the maximum allowable level. Specifically, if your 401(k) plan offers to match part of your contributions, make the needed contributions. Why leave free money on the table?

There's a big difference between deliberate borrowing and being in debt. The borrower is comfortable because he or she has ample capacity to repay and, most important, decides or controls the timing of repayment. The debtor borrows only what a lender decides to lend and must repay at the time chosen by the lender. That's why borrowing with a mortgage is very different from "being in debt." (Just as borrowing differs from being in debt, retirement differs from old age. In retirement you have more time for travel, reading, sports, and other interests. In old age your body aches in different ways every day. And every night.)

Figure 18.3 tells an important story about inflation. The figures in the second row, labeled "Nest-egg goal," are the amounts you would need to have saved by age 65 to have the inflation-adjusted equivalent of $35,000 in yearly spending money. (If you want $70,000 a year of spending money to sustain your lifestyle, multiply the figures in the second row by 2; if you want $105,000, multiply by 3, and so on.) Here's how to read the table:

- Find your present age in the top row.
- The nest-egg goal is the amount of capital you will need to accumulate to have an inflation-adjusted $35,000 to spend each year from age 65 on.
- The current savings on the left—ranging from $0 to $250,000—is the annual amount invested tax-free at a return of 10 percent annually until you reach age 65.

- The rest of the table shows which of those amounts you would need to save and invest to achieve your nest-egg goal.
- After retirement at age 65, the assumed returns average 7 percent. And at age 90, it is further assumed, all your accumulated savings will have been spent.

Your current age Nest-egg goal	25 $3 mil.	30 $2.5 mil.	35 $2.1 mil.	40 $1.7 mil.	45 $1.4 mil.	50 $1.1 mil.	55 $.94 mil.
Your current savings	How much you need to save annually						
$ 0	$6,890	$9,248	$12,524	$17,217	$24,300	$36,004	$58,995
$ 10,000	$5,868	$8,211	$11,463	$16,116	$23,125	$34,689	$57,367
$ 25,000	$4,334	$6,656	$ 9,872	$14,463	$21,363	$32,717	$54,926
$ 50,000	$1,777	$4,064	$ 7,220	$11,709	$18,427	$29,430	$50,857
$100,000	$ 0	$ 0	$ 1,916	$ 6,201	$12,554	$22,856	$42,720
$250,000	$ 0	$ 0	$ 0	$ 0	$ 0	$ 3,315	$18,308

Figure 18.3 What it will take to get to there from here

Look at Figure 18.3 again. If you are age 30 (the second column), you'll need to accumulate $2.5 million by the time you reach age 65 to produce $35,000 a year of real spending money. The column shows—for each level of savings you've already accumulated—how much you'll have to save every year to achieve that goal.

Note the rather favorable assumptions: All your savings go into a tax-deferred account such as a 401(k) plan, where they are further assumed to compound at 10 percent annually until your retirement at age 65. Starting from present market levels, this may be possible but will not be easy—even if you invest entirely in equities. In bonds, it simply cannot be done.

Remember algebra and solving equations with two unknowns? Did your course get to three unknowns? As investors, we are confronted by a much more complex challenge: to solve, or at least manage sensibly and rationally, a puzzle with five major unknowns, each of which is changing. The five unknowns are:

- Rate of return on investments
- Inflation
- Spending
- Taxes
- Time

One analysis of three dozen years' experience (from 1964 to 2000) starts with the happy assumption that an investor began with a cool $1 million.[1] The consequences of various investment programs are then examined. The nominal compound rates of return for this period were apparently quite encouraging: 11.8 percent for stocks, 7.9 percent for bonds, and 6.8 percent for Treasury bills (or cash equivalents). The very pleasing—but, as we'll soon see, very deceptive—*theoretical final portfolio values* produced by the initial $1 million were as follows:

Stocks	$55.0 million
Bonds	$15.5 million
T-bills	$10.7 million

Everyone's a winner! Or so it may appear. But here's *how the results look after taxes:*

Stocks	$30.2 million
Bonds	$ 6.6 million
T-bills	$ 4.4 million

What a difference those taxes make—particularly to bonds and T-bills. Note that the taxes assumed are minimal: The investor pays only federal taxes (no state or local taxes), has no other sources of taxable income, and files a joint return. For most investors who can invest $1 million, actual taxes are almost certain to be larger.[2]

Brace yourself for the impact of inflation, because that's the way we convert nominal or apparent values into real money. The results are sobering. Here's *the result after adjusting for inflation* over the same 35 years:

Stocks	$5.4 million
Bonds	$1.2 million
T-bills	$0.8 million

Inflation, the data show, is a far larger problem for investors than taxes. In real purchasing power, bonds are only 20 percent ahead of the initial investment after a whole generation.[3] And T-bills are actually behind the starting line by 20 percent. That's why taxes and inflation are rightly known as "fearsome fiscal pirates."

It would be worse if the study had included realistic ownership costs such as mutual fund expenses and trading costs. Even the typical money market mutual fund charges roughly 0.5 percent per year in expenses, while bond funds charge up to 1 percent, and stock funds can charge as much as 1.5 percent. At those rates, you would have the following take-home *results after deducting ownership costs:*

Stocks	$1.8 million
Bonds	$755,000
T-bills	$589,000

Finally, as all investors were painfully reminded in 2008–2009, to earn the long-term "average" return, you would have had to have enough fortitude to stay fully invested when the market dropped and inflation was tearing away at your portfolio—and your confidence and determination to stay the course were surely faltering.

Spending is the next key factor. Again, time makes all the difference. Consider the consequences of two commonly used spending rules. One spending rule is "to limit spending in retirement to a moderate rate such as 5 percent of your capital." If you followed this spending rule, and your investments were entirely in bonds, your $1 million would have fallen in real money—purchasing power—to just $200,000. The all-stock portfolio alternative is better, of course, but not by much. It would be up by about 30 percent—less than 1 percent per year.

Another spending rule is "to limit spending to cash income (that is, the investor spends only the cash income of a portfolio) as dividends and interest payments are received." The investor following this rule starts out having significantly less to spend than does Mr. 5 Percent but, because dividends rise with corporate earnings, soon catches up and goes ahead in spending more. Compounding is at work again.

Beware of a subtle danger. As an investor you can almost always produce more income from your portfolio by investing more and more heavily in bonds or so-called income stocks with high dividend yields. But other investors are rational, and they'll let *you* get more today only if *they* can expect more tomorrow.[4] Thus, part of what appears to be high current income is really a return of capital. For example, high-yield bonds may appear to pay 8 to 10 percent interest, but part of that payment is actually a return of capital—the capital that's needed to offset occasional defaults. And every so often, one of those high-yield bonds does default.

What to do? In retirement, be conservative—better safe than sorry. Limit annual withdrawals to 4 percent of a three-year moving average of your portfolio. This will protect your portfolio from inflation *and* from overspending. If you need to draw 5 percent each year, you'll want more stability. Put a rolling five years' expenditures in medium-term bonds and the rest in equities the year you retire. Each year, convert one more year's spending from equities to bonds *unless* the market is high and all the chatter is about good prospects—in which case, you'll be wise to convert *two* years; if the chatter is about *great* prospects, convert *three*. Yes, this *is* a form of market timing, but it's seldom a bad idea to lean against the wind.

If you need to draw up to 6 percent of your retirement funds to live comfortably, you need to know you will be depleting your capital over time after adjusting for inflation—and eventually you *will* run out of money. If 6 percent won't meet your spending level, you owe it to yourself to cut back your spending to a level you can sustain. Nobody wants to outlive his or her resources.

Money links the past with the present and the present with the future as a medium of stored value. You can estimate the dollars you'll want to spend each year and, at a spending rate such as 4 percent, the total wealth required to produce the income to meet that level of spending. Determine what you have now and what you will save each year. Then see whether you can achieve your capital-accumulation objectives through a sensible investing program. If the first plan you design doesn't "work," you go around again, planning to save more each year or work and save for more years *or* have less to live on. Be careful: Being optimistic will not help. Be cautious and conservative with each assumption: your saving rate, your rate of return, and your spending assumptions.

For investors who depend on their annual income from investments, the good news is that while interest paid on T-bills will fluctuate from year to year, sometimes substantially, dividends on a portfolio of common stocks have almost never gone down and will generally rise at approximately the rate of inflation.

By combining your saving and capital objectives with your realistic rate-of-return expectations and your available time horizon, you can work out your own investor's triangulation to see what amount of savings you will need to contribute each year to your long-term investments to successfully achieve your realistic objectives for spendable money during retirement. Your accountant or investment advisor can help you with the calculations.

If you're surprised at how much you'll need to save and invest each year to meet your retirement goals, it may be modestly comforting to know that you are not alone. Retirement is expensive, partly because we live longer than did our parents or grandparents (and incur more medical expenses in our later years), but primarily because inflation is such a powerful and unrelenting opponent.

Investors may ponder the double-edged irony of death. If death comes sooner than expected and planned for, the resources saved over many years may go, at least partially, unused by the saver. If death comes much later than planned for, the saved-up resources may be too small, and a grim poverty can result. Be prudent, but don't be prudent to excess. You can save too much, and those who love you do not want you to suffer a life of self-enforced poverty so that they can have extra money to spend after you're gone.

The best bargain for a long-term investor is to obtain sound investment counseling that leads to the sensible long-term investing program that is most appropriate to that investor. Ironically, most investors do not seek—and are unwilling to pay for—real help in developing an optimal long-term investment program. This grievous sin of omission incurs great opportunity cost: the cost of missing out on what might easily have been.

Most investors could obtain very good investment counseling from a major fund company for a fee of less than $1,000 (paid only once each decade). Most investors will regularly pay more than $10,000 per million dollars every year in investment operating expenses such as brokerage commissions, advisory fees, and custody expenses. It's ironic that investors will, however innocently, pay more for the lesser value.

PLANNING YOUR PLAY *155*

Suggestion: Pick one day a year (for example, your birthday, New Year's Day, or Thanksgiving) as your "day away for investing" and pledge to spend a few hours on that day every year quietly and systematically answering the following questions in writing. (After the first annual review, which may take several hours, you'll be updating the plan you wrote out in the prior year, and so it won't take more than an hour or so. You can make that hour even more productive by rereading last year's plan a week or so before your "day away" so it will be in your subconscious, where so much good thinking and rethinking gets done.) These questions will help define and articulate your objectives:

- During retirement, how much income do I want to have each year in addition to Social Security and my employer's retirement benefit?
- How many years will I be in retirement? (The key here is to estimate how long you'll live. Ask your doctor how to apply the average life span of your parents or grandparents to get a reasonable fix on your own "genetic envelope," appropriately adjusted for the healthfulness of your personal lifestyle.)
- What spending rule am I ready to live with and live by?
- How much capital will I need to provide amply for retirement?
- What insurance will I need—inflation-adjusted—to cover full health care for my spouse and me?
- How much capital do I want to pass on to each member of my family and to any special friends?
- How much capital do I wish to direct to my philanthropic priorities?

Next comes an easy-to-use solution to what most investors consider the truly difficult part of the problem: estimating long-term average annual rates of return on your investments. Here's one way.

First, recognize that over the long, long term—after adjusting for inflation—average returns for each type of investment have been approximately as follows:

Stocks	4.5 percent
Bonds	1.5 percent
T-bills	1.25 percent

If you are operating on the assumption that you can get long-term real returns of 10 percent a year from stocks, you are surely being way too optimistic.

Second, remember and act on the understanding that over the truly long term, the most important investment decisions seem almost obvious. Here are the two most important decision rules: Any funds that will stay invested for 10 years or longer should be in stocks. Any funds that will be invested for less than two to three years should be in "cash" or money market instruments.

Your next step is to prepare a complete inventory of your investment assets, including the following: investments in stocks and bonds, equity in your home, and assets in any retirement plans, including IRAs, Keoghs, and 401(k) or 403(b) plans.

Next, review your retirement income. (You can get help from your employer's human resources department or from your accountant.) Here are the obvious sources: pension benefits, Social Security, and income from your investments.

Next come your desired bequests to family members (and others) and intended charitable contributions.

In investing over the longer run, benign neglect really does pay off. After basic decisions on long-term investment policy have been made with care and rigor, you should—with great respect—hold onto them. The problem, as Shakespeare knew, lies not in our stars but in ourselves, so above all else, resist the insidious temptation to do something. "Nervous money never wins," say poker players. And they know. At the Kinderheim nursery in Vail, Colorado, the experience-based sign offers skiers a fine service at a great price: "Leave your kids for the day: $5." Then, mindful of past experience with overanxious parents, two "alternatives" are offered: "You watch: $10" and "You help: $25."

One final thought: Before making any commitments that are large in proportion to total wealth, the investor would be wise to reread *King Lear*.

End Notes

1. AllianceBernstein, pp. 5–16.
2. The effective tax rate on stocks is far lower than the effective tax rate on bonds because part of the return on stocks is market appreciation; the capital gains tax rate is lower and payment is often deferred for many years—until you decide to sell. A reasonable estimate of the actual or effective federal tax rate on returns from stocks is under 20 percent, about half the tax rate on income from bonds or bills.
3. Note that in all but one year since 1950, if you invested in tax-free municipal bonds and then held and reinvested for 20 years, you lost. In that one favorable initial investment year, you made 0.01 percent annually after inflation, but before management or custody expenses.
4. The market is a place for best exchanges where people will let you have more of what you want if—and only if—you let them get more of what they want.

CHAPTER 19

DISASTER—AGAIN

O N DECEMBER 11, 2008, 8,000 INVESTORS—FORMERLY HAPPY
to be receiving reports of their year-in–year-out returns of
10 percent or better on a secretive "inside the market" operation
they had been privately let in on by well-connected friends—
found they had actually been victims of a giant Ponzi scheme run
by Bernard L. Madoff.

Madoff said that he specialized in "split-strike conversion"
strategies using derivatives to minimize risk, which he made
clear were so proprietary that he would not discuss them in any
detail for fear others would copy his technique and ruin everything for everyone. He claimed to buy stocks and sell put and
call options on them. (Selling the calls would mean not partici-
pating in a price increase beyond a set amount, while the puts
were to protect against a price decrease by a set amount.) To protect his secret process, Madoff, a market titan who had been
chairman of Nasdaq, kept a tight inner circle, having audits done
by a tiny three-person accounting firm and all trading executed
through his own captive dealership.

Like Charles Ponzi in the 1920s, Madoff had been paying out
money to withdrawing investors not from accumulating profits but
from new cash coming in from new investors. Those content to
receive 10 percent or so *every* year—at which rate, money doubles

in just over seven years and doubles again in the next seven *and* doubles again—got comforting monthly reports on how steadily their fortunes were compounding. Most preferred to leave their money with Madoff, presumably multiplying steadily. Consistency was remarkable: only 11 monthly losses from 1992 to 2008.

The lesson for all: If it seems too good to believe and "this time it's different," it *is* too good to be believed. So don't. Sure, Bernie was charming, modest, and bright. Sure, it was a family firm. Sure, you got introduced through a friend of a friend. Sure, you felt sure you could trust him. Everybody seemed to. Ten percent was very good—good enough to attract investors—but not beyond plausibility. The Securities and Exchange Commission (SEC) had been "tipped" several times, but had not found any wrongdoing. Bernie had friends in a variety of charities and in other high places.

Fifty billion dollars was Madoff's initial estimate—later corrected to seventy-five billion—of how much money he had vaporized. For Madoff's victims it was a disaster. Their money would never come back.

* * * * *

On October 6, 2008, Iceland, geographically remote near the Arctic Circle and historically detached from the rest of the world, with a hardy population of just 320,000, became the epicenter of financial violence. Icelanders, traditionally savers and famously stubborn after enduring serial hardships, had a national pension system sufficient to ensure security to all their elderly. All that suddenly changed when Prime Minister Geir Haarde went on TV to make two astonishing announcements: The nation was virtually bankrupt, and the government was taking over all three banks.

In the years before Haarde's painful broadcast, Iceland's bold, self-congratulating young businessmen, who called themselves Viking Raiders, had borrowed heavily to acquire companies— and big private jets and British football clubs. But suddenly all lending had stopped cold, currency exchange was not possible, the nation was bankrupt, and the three banks were bankrupt as were were many Icelandic families and businesses.

Iceland's krona was frozen in the world's capital markets. Easy access to loans and 100 percent mortgages—payable in foreign currencies *and* ominously indexed to inflation that had shot up to 20 percent annually—had enabled young people to buy homes, cars, and furniture with debt. Retirement funds that had been sufficient to ensure security for all were suddenly cut in half—then cut even more.

In the seven years after the national banks had been privatized, Iceland's financial institutions had borrowed $75 billion abroad—many times the national Gross Domestic Product (GDP) and $250,000 for every person in Iceland. (By comparison, America's horrendous $700 billion financial rescue package was "only" 5 percent of GDP.) Some blamed the Viking Raiders, some blamed lax regulators. Never before had any nation, or any country's population, been trapped so cataclysmically in the stark realities of being deeply mired in debt to strangers.

That's why the head of government went on television to address the nation: "Fellow countrymen . . . If there was ever a time when the Icelandic nation needed to stand together and show fortitude in the face of adversity, then this is the moment. I urge you all to guard that which is most important in the life of every one of us, to protect those values which will survive the storm now beginning. I urge families to talk together and not allow anxiety to get the upper hand, even though the outlook is grim for many. We need to explain to our children that the world is not on the edge of a precipice, and we all need to find an inner courage to look to the future. . . . Thus, with Icelandic optimism, fortitude, and solidarity as weapons, we will ride out the storm. God bless Iceland." All across Iceland, silence followed.

There was no sympathy for Iceland or its banks when 500,000 British and continental savers—individuals, charities, and local authorities—realized that they had just lost $15 billion, or an average of $30,000 per loser. Restoring those losses would take longer than most listeners' lifetimes.

* * * * *

The Madoff and Iceland experiences are both different in one profound way from the global market meltdown of 2008. Both losses were permanent, gone forever. Markets, on the other hand, do recover, so the great risk to individual investors is not that the market can plummet, but that the investor may be frightened into liquidating his or her investments at or near the bottom and miss all the recovery, making the loss permanent. This happens to all too many investors in every terrible market drop.

Market prices, as we all know, are driven by buying and selling. The only way to push prices up to peak levels is for the largest possible number of investors with the most money—including borrowed money—to reach their highest conviction that stocks are an imperative "buy." And the only way to drive prices down to their lowest level is to have the largest possible aggregate amount of insistent, concentrated selling. That's what happened all over the world in the fall of 2008.

It had all started with high levels of confidence in the outlook for the economy and corporate profits and a highly confident view that risk was low. In stock market after stock market around the world, prices were between "fully priced" and "high." There were few bargains. Those prices might have been okay if the underlying economies and corporate earnings had continued to advance. But in one of the sharpest-ever reversals of expectation, investors, banks, individuals, and governments—the world's financial system, which had been financing expansion with debt—slammed into reverse.

Trust disappeared, taking credit with it. The culprit at the center was the ever-increasing use of leverage, particularly in the United States. Easy credit terms, low interest rates, derivatives, the increasing mass of leveraged hedge funds, and the SEC's authorizing Wall Street dealers to increase their use of debt were major ingredients in the cheap credit cocktail. Republicans, determined to deregulate the economy, joined forces with Democrats interested in enabling more families to get mortgages; they acted to change the home-loan regulations and increase credit from Fannie Mae and Freddie Mac, leading eventually to "ninja" loans to borrowers with *no income, no jobs,* and no *assets* who had assumed they could speculate profitably on rising house prices. Packages of inappropriate mortgage loans were securitized and sold all over the world. When their values plunged, the pain was everywhere, particularly through credit default insurance, which proved to be disastrously underwritten.

Economic, market, and psychological dominoes pushed each other over. Confidence disappeared. Credit ratings were found faulty, and security values were cut. Credit markets froze up. Leverage was pulled away from hedge funds and dealers. Credit markets stayed frozen. Prominent financial institutions failed. Government rescues collided with election-eve politics. Forced selling and anticipation of more hard selling dominated markets that were already dropping because of fears of recession. In 14 months, the U.S. stock market lost *half* its value—more than $7 trillion. Yet the pain, awful as it was, was not as great—inflation-adjusted— as it was in the 1970s. (See Chapter 18.)

Credit rating agencies were severely criticized for failing to understand the true creditworthiness of the securities, particularly packaged subprime loans, that they had been rating AAA. Great corporations like GE could not even refinance short-term commercial paper, and Lehman Brothers was allowed to fail, thus roiling credit markets severely. Wachovia and Washington Mutual went into shotgun mergers. AIG, the largest insurance company, was taken over by the government. Comparable difficulties beset commercial banks, central banks, and governments in one nation after another.

Wall Street's prime brokers insisted that hedge funds sharply reduce their use of margin debt. Investor withdrawals from these funds compounded the selling pressure. Massive, urgent selling swept into the markets as hedge funds and others dumped stocks to raise cash to meet lenders' insistent demands and in anticipation of a further drop in share prices.

The sudden traumatic break in the stock markets of the world forced investors to answer the hard question: Now what?

The "now what?" question every investor was asking would bring a new clarity to the true meaning of risk. In its classic and most powerful definition, risk is a function of unacceptable *permanent* loss. Madoff and Iceland exemplified that kind of risk. So too did the destruction of Lehman Brothers and others. And so did individual investors who sold off their stocks in the late fall of 2008 in a "flight to safety," making their personal market disasters permanent. For long-term investors, as always, the worst action would be getting out of stocks. But, as always, that's what many investors would do: Lock the barn door *after* the animals had run off. In the jargon of Wall Street, this was a *big* "black swan" event—black swans being creatures that, though rare, do show themselves once in a while.

After this debacle, two defensible actions for an investor would be either to rebalance to the long-term optimal asset mix or, recognizing that the magnitude of the drop in equity prices was so large, to overweight equities.

For investors who accept the logic of investing for the long term in equities, the sudden drop was a combination of four forces:

- Debt leverage in the markets and among consumers had reached unsustainable record levels.
- Stocks had been somewhat overpriced—"ahead of themselves"—and were due for a 10 percent correction even if the economy continued on.

- Recognition that the global economy, and particularly the U.S. economy, were going into a serious recession would explain another 20 to 30 percent downward revision in "fair value."
- Traders' anticipation of acute selling pressure resulting from sudden demands for deleveraging and market uncertainties could easily explain a bear market price cut of another 10 to 20 percent.

Investors taking such a view and maintaining a long-term discipline in their thinking could have concluded that, stunning as the total certainly was, these components, taken individually, were not as frightening as their total effect.

The next question investors might ask was far harder to answer: Why did so few see the giant black swan approaching? There the lesson for long-term investors is that in rising markets most prices are set by optimists and tend to be high; investors are optimistic in part because they do not study the negatives, particularly new or game-changing negatives.

For very long-term investors, the giant market losses were not a lasting disaster, but they certainly were painful. And there was a plethora of disasters for certain individuals, such as scholarship students who, given the drop in endowments, could not get the larger scholarship they needed when one of their parents lost a job and had to drop out or shift down to a lesser school. Others lost their jobs and began spending down their savings—all too often liquidating stocks at low prices. As unemployment crept up toward 10 percent, the symptoms of societal illness—domestic violence, divorce, suicide, drunk driving, burglary, and child abuse—began to escalate. As usual, much of the pain and anguish were experienced personally and in private.

And it was at least a partial disaster for people who had retired in prior years, confident they had enough in their 401(k) plans to live comfortably in retirement and who now suddenly did not have enough. As recession spread, the large drop in the stock market combined with extensive and extended layoffs and over-all uncertainty to cast a very dark shadow over our economy and our society.

Once again, we were learning to recognize and respect the power of economic laws and the reality that the greatest risks are created by increasing numbers of people coming to believe that risk has been brought under control and that this time it's differ-ent. It's never different because what people see—like the shad-ows on the wall in Plato's cave—is always a reflection of themselves.

Readers may wonder whether the dramatic lessons of 2008 have changed any of my basic beliefs. Certainly, as with most investors and full-time observers of the capital markets, it's no excuse to say that I recognized that subprime mortgage lending made no sense for either borrowers or lenders. I knew that credit card debt was dangerous and believed deeply that federal deficits were a national disgrace. I urged everyone to get out of debt and to be conservative in investments. But that was not enough—not nearly enough.

I feel chagrined not to have recognized the magnitude and extent of the problems or the severity of the markets' reaction or the magnitude of required government intervention. And it's all too small comfort to know that almost every professional investor was also surprised. That said, having the opportunity to reeval-uate every aspect of this book's message, I return to the advice Ben Graham and Dave Dodd gave in their 1934 classic *Security Analysis*: "Long term investors should guard against learning too much from the adversities of recent experience."

In nearly 50 years of experience and learning about investing from outstanding practitioners and expert theorists around the world, I've tried to collect, distill, and explain as clearly and plainly as possible the principles for successful investing. While I'm increasingly impressed by how much detail is neither known nor knowable, I've become increasingly comfortable with the thought that for individual investors who wish to win the loser's game and have the necessary self-discipline, the simple messages in this short book are now and will be the keys to success for the *next* 50 years.

CHAPTER 20

ENDGAME

INVESTORS CAN—AND CERTAINLY SHOULD—SUBSTANTIALLY increase their lifetime financial and emotional success by paying appropriate attention to what chess players know is important: the endgame.

If you are fortunate, as many Americans are, to have earned or inherited more than you need to live out your own definition of the good life, you'll have the opportunity *and* the responsibility to decide where and how to direct the funds not spent. Most affluent people focus on two quite different kinds of beneficiaries that can both be deeply meaningful: people (usually family members) and values (usually such philanthropic organizations as colleges, schools, hospitals, and religious organizations).

Deciding what will be done with your capital to maximize its real value can be just as important as deciding how to save, accumulate, and invest it. Providing for your retirement is one of three important challenges and opportunities. Bequests and gifts to those you love is another. The third—"giving back" to society— can be exciting and fulfilling.

Since money is such an effective way to store or transfer value, an investor with a surplus beyond his or her own lifetime's wants and needs will have the opportunity to make a difference to others. Blessed is the investor whose assets do good; cursed are those who, despite their best intentions, cause harm. Many cause harm.

Wealth *is* power—both the power to do good and the power to do harm. Greater wealth means greater power. Investors who have enjoyed substantial financial success should give careful consideration—no matter what their hopes or intentions—to whether the amount of wealth they can transfer to their children might do real harm by distorting their offspring's values and priorities or by taking away their descendants' joy of making their own way in life. As we know, all too often poor little rich kids *are* miserable. While Mae West was speaking for herself when she announced that "too much of a good thing can be *wunnerful*," a giant inheritance is usually not wonderful for your children.

"Successful families make thoughtful choices concerning their wealth and think about the effect of their decisions on the lives of their children and their spouses and their grandchildren," says Harvard's senior philanthropic advisor, Charles Collier. "Most importantly, they talk openly with their children, at age-appropriate times, about all the issues surrounding the four components of the family's true wealth and give their younger family members as much responsibility as they can manage as soon as possible."

As Collier explains: "According to Aristotle and his latter-day student, Thomas Jefferson, the 'pursuit of happiness' has to do with an internal journey to know ourselves and an external journey of service of others."

Before outlining some of the possibilities for transfers within the circle of those you love or feel responsibility for, let's remember that money has powerful symbolic meaning. Psychiatrists marvel that while patients talk rather extensively and relatively early in therapy about relationships with parents, childhood experiences, central hopes and fears, and even very private matters such as dreams and sexual experiences, the one subject almost never discussed is money.

Most people find it very difficult to discuss money matters openly, fully, rationally, and wisely. Therefore, it's best to be especially thoughtful and cautious when making plans about how your money will pass on to others. Yes, it's your money now and while you live—but neither of these cheerful current realities will last forever. Money is often the thermonuclear device among symbols, and it symbolizes a lot—in different ways for different people, often in quite unexpected ways.

You'll want to get expert legal advice when formulating a sound estate plan, but here are some items for consideration, recognizing that each person will have his or her own objectives and resources and will want to make his or her own decisions:

1. Everyone who qualifies for an individual retirement account (IRA) should have one. And everyone who can possibly afford to do so should contribute the maximum every year, enabling the twin engines of long-term compounding and tax deferral to do their magic. The annual maximum is $5,000, or $6,000 for people 50 and above; both will be indexed to inflation after 2009.

   Get your children or grandchildren started early. Once they begin earning income on their own, you can give an IRA contribution of up to $5,000 per year to each child or grandchild—up to the amount of their earned income.
2. You can give up to $13,000—without tax—to *each* person you wish *every* year. Married couples can give $26,000 annually to each person. For most investors over time these annual gifts can be a central, even dominant part of a lifelong estate planning and family investment management program. (Gifts to young children can be made in care of a parent as custodian under the Uniform Transfers to Minors Act.) One

main advantage of these gifts lies in completely sidestepping the estate tax when you die.

You might concentrate on your children. Such gifts can really mount up, partly because the future investment income earned on the sums given is taxed at the child's tax rate, which is almost certain to be far lower than yours. Over 20 years, $13,000 given annually can, with sensible investing, accumulate to the better part of $500,000; $26,000 a year from both parents could produce $1 million or more. Again, the keys to success are *time* and *compounding*, so plan well, start early, and stay with your plan.

3. You have a lifetime total limit of $1 million on other tax-free gifts to individuals. If you have sufficient capital, a serious look at estate tax tables—particularly at the highest incremental rate you're likely to incur—will strongly encourage you to use this right to give. And contemplation of the cumulative consequences of compound interest will encourage you to exercise this right relatively early in life.

4. Despite Elizabethan laws against "perpetuities," the IRS allows you to put up to $1 million into a generation-skipping tax-free family fund. (Your children can decide how this trust's assets will be divided among their descendants.) Gift or estate taxes must be paid *before* the assets pass to this fund. However, once this initial tax is paid, the assets can grow and accumulate tax-free for several generations within your family, typically for up to 80 to 100 years. Remember that if investments increase by 7 percent per annum after income tax, they will double every 10 years, so $1 million can become $1 billion in 100 years (before adjusting for inflation). In the meantime, this family fund can operate as a family bank by allowing distributions or loans to family members as needed.

5. A curious provision called a "qualified personal residence trust" enables you to transfer ownership of your house to your children and live in your home rent-free for a period of time (such as 15 years). You save substantially on estate taxes—unless you die before the trust matures—while ownership passes to your children.

A home can be transferred as a taxable gift valued at only 20 to 30 percent of the current market value. The IRS considers the taxable present value of the gift to be just the value of the children's right to take possession at the end of, say, the 15-year term of the trust. (The discount to a low present value is the obverse of the powerful accumulation or growth generated by compound interest.)

6. If you wish to transfer substantial sums to your descendants but you worry about distorting their values and lives with too much money at too early an age—before they reach "fiscal maturity"—consider an arrangement proposed by Jackie Onassis (but reversed by her children under an optional provision in her will that you can leave out of yours).

Here's the general idea: A trust can be established for 20 to 30 years with interim annual distributions of income payable to your favorite school or charity (either at a set dollar amount or as a percentage of the trust's assets), with the trust corpus (the principal or main body of the money, from the Latin word for "body") paid after the 20- to 30-year term to your chosen beneficiaries, such as your children. There's no estate tax, and a gift tax is paid only on the estimated net present value of the trust's corpus after discounting at the IRS's prescribed interest rate—an amount that is only a fraction of the probable market value of the corpus 20 to 30 years from now.

If you are concerned about the harm that might be done by a *current* wealth transfer to a 30- to 35-year-old beneficiary, but are sanguine that the same transfer in the *future* would not harm the values of that same person at age 60 or 65, this sort of trust can be an effective way to transfer substantial wealth with minimal tax. Noting that the key figures are all based on estimates of market valuations far in the future, the wise investor will want to work out the specific term of the trust and the investment policy under several different scenarios and select the choice with which he or she feels most comfortable.

7. It takes more capital to deliver $1 million after taxes as a bequest ($2.2 million) than as a gift ($1.55 million). Gift taxes are assessed on the gift without regard to other taxes paid, while estate taxes are based on the whole estate before taxes are deducted.

8. Curiously, and quite accurately, estate lawyers will advise that one of the best assets to use for charitable giving at your death may be your currently tax-exempt defined contribution retirement fund: 401(k), 403(b), IRA, or profit-sharing plan. This surprising anomaly is true because these assets must be included in your estate—subject not only to the estate tax but also to income taxes as distributions are paid out to beneficiaries as of your date of death. Both of these taxes can be avoided if you decide to donate the capital to charity.

Inverted or upside-down reasoning can be a usefully mind-freeing way to explore any complex issue. Investors can think of estate taxes not as a tax on *wealth* but as a tax on *caution*—your reluctance to make irrevocable decisions while living (particularly long, long before your death) about the distribution of your wealth. If you are willing and able to make irrevocable decisions now regarding the long-term future disposition of your capital, you can save substantially on taxes. And, as always, a penny saved is a penny earned.

Most investors are *not* willing to make these wealth-distribution decisions—yet. But please remember: Only if you are willing to make decisions about the future now can the power of compound interest be used for the maximum period to have the maximum impact on achieving your carefully considered goals and objectives. Claude N. Rosenberg, in addition to authoring several good books on how to make money in investing, wrote *Wealthy and Wise,* a pioneering book on how to think through what you can afford to give to others. Claude's analysis shows that most people could be much more generous than they seem to realize.

Maximizing your lifetime financial success has five stages or dimensions:

- Earning
- Saving
- Investing
- Contributing
- Estate planning

Ideally, you will maximize achievement in each area—according to your own values—within the feasible set of opportunities available to you as you enjoy a full and balanced life.

As with other areas of investing, it's wise to plan ahead, to be conservative (within limits), and to make productive use of time by beginning early and sustaining your commitments over as long a period as you can.

Education is usually your best investment, whether you invest in your own education or the education of your children or grandchildren—or in educating a great kid whose family can't afford the education of his or her choice. Education increases earning power—for years and years—and leads to richer, more enjoyably interesting lives with more freedom of choice. The other "best investment" is staying in good health through exercise, weight control, not smoking, and the like. You really can live longer and better—and at lower total cost.

Investors who have conscientiously worked to *maximize* the amount of their savings and investments will also want to pay comparable attention to *minimizing* the diversion of funds caused by taxes, particularly estate taxes. This effort will help maximize the amount of funds devoted to achieving your desired fiscal objectives in support of your values.

In thinking about bequests to children and grandchildren, wise people focus on deciding what amount would be best—as in enough. Consider, please, the following poetic doorway to wisdom from Kurt Vonnegut:

True story, word of honor. Joseph Heller, an important and funny writer, now dead, and I were at a party given by a billionaire on Shelter Island.

I said, "Joe, how does it make you feel to know that our host only yesterday may have made more money than your novel *Catch-22* has earned in its entire history?" And Joe said, "I've got something he can never have." And I said, "What on earth could that be, Joe?" And Joe said, "The knowledge that I've got enough."

Not bad! Rest in peace!

Two of the wealthiest people in the United States have decided to leave only moderate amounts to their children. Warren Buffett says that[1] the perfect amount to leave children is "enough money so they would feel they could do anything, but not so much that they could do nothing." Buffett's friend Bill Gates echoes that view. "Part of the reason for believing that my wealth should be given back to society," says Gates, "and not in any substantial percentage be passed on to my children, is that I don't think it would be good for them. They really need to get out and work and contribute to society. I think that's an important element of a fulfilling life."

When thinking about gifts and bequests to children, parents know that each child is an individual and may be quite different from siblings in wealth, earnings, or financial needs. This can make it tough to decide between "fair" and "equal."

The best financial plans resolve the natural tension or dynamic between each person being an individual and each being part of a family. Capital transfers can divide or enhance family relationships. What's right for taxes may or may not be right for the individuals in your family.

Most families have core values—such as philanthropy or entrepreneurship—that need money for realization. Sharing and developing those values can be an important part of the next generation's growing-up years. The meaning you give to wealth says a lot about who you are and the way you'll be seen and remembered. That's why developing shared values with your family and articulating guiding principles that will inform your family's choices can be so important. *Suggestion*: Take time to "introduce" your will with a page or more telling those you love your values and feelings. It may be your last opportunity to be heard.[2] If you have surplus funds beyond the amount you wish to transfer to members of your family and others you care for, don't overlook the profoundly rewarding opportunities you may have created for yourself to cause good things to happen through philanthropy.

"Giving money away to charity" puts the whole proposition the wrong way. Instead, think in terms of imaginatively and vigorously *investing* your money—the stored values you and your skills have created over many years—to make good things happen for and through the people and organizations you care about. You can derive a great deal of pleasure and personal fulfillment in the process of making a positive difference in other people's lives.

People inclined to think they have made their fortunes by themselves are partly right. Most fortune builders *did* work hard, did take risks, and did overcome major barriers. Still, they might well ponder how well they would have done if they had been born in central Africa or western China, or a variety of other places. Most Americans know that they owe a large fraction of their success to our dynamic economy and its myriad market opportunities, our educational system, and the ability to let investment values compound without tax until they are sold and then to pay only capital gains taxes.

No man or woman is an island; as John Donne understood, we are all part of the main. Those with modest wealth may focus on their families and a few local charities, while those with more wealth may respond to the family of humanity and their opportunities to invest wealth creatively in reducing painful problems or increasing opportunities. On Abraham Maslow's famous "needs hierarchy," after and above "self-actualization" are *transcendences*. These needs can be realized when we move beyond ourselves to see fulfillment as linked directly to serving the needs and hopes of others.

Givers have learned how greatly they can enjoy seeing the wealth they have created—the stored-up consequences of their hard work, imagination, and good fortune—come to life *again* by reducing constraints on individuals or society and enabling good things to happen during their lives in ways that matter to them. As the old saying has it, "you can't take it with you." Those who give something back invariably speak of this dimension of their lives with genuine satisfaction. And those who contribute more find they enjoy even greater satisfaction.

Select the actions or changes that would give you deep spiritual satisfaction or pleasure to see coming to fruition, and make these good things come true by committing your capital to help make them happen. Like many others, you may find you enjoy great gratification in converting your financial resources into actions and values you truly care about. Here are some opportunities to consider that will help you make an impact:

- Establish scholarships for young people with great talent who aspire to make significant contributions in the arts, science, or business.
- Contribute to scholarships for young people who've gotten a bad deal in life and need someone's help to get on the right road. (If you don't have a particular school in mind, consider Berea College, which accepts *only* kids who can't afford a college education.)
- Provide financial support for advancing science, medicine, or social justice.
- Support hospitals, shelters, and other institutions to help those in severe need.
- Help make your community a better place to live in by being one of the "go-to" leaders who commits time and money to make good things happen.
- Supply funding for the arts—music, dance, theater, painting, sculpture—that enrich our lives.

Your greatest satisfaction may come from serving a major national institution, a global organization, or a small entity in your neighborhood. Experienced charitable activists agree that while contributing money is important, even greater enjoyment and satisfaction result when they also make a substantial commitment of their time, skills, and energy. Don't leave this important part of your life experience "in storage" in the attic or the bank—for someone else to enjoy doing after you're gone.

One of my personal "light bulbs" lit up while I was enjoying clams at Charley O's restaurant in Rockefeller Center in 1974. Huge black-and-white photographs of movie stars decorated the walls; each had a one-line quote under the picture. The movie star looming over my table was the once very dissolute Tasmanian swashbuckler Errol Flynn. His quote: "Any guy who dies with more than 10 grand has made a mistake." While Flynn surely had other things on his mind, I resolved there and then to avoid the mistake of paying more than necessary in estate taxes by giving during my lifetime. I prefer to make some errors of *commission* (giving to causes that later disappoint) than to make errors of *omission* (giving too little or too late). It's been interesting and fun—and very rewarding.

Contributing your time, talent, and money can be profoundly gratifying in two ways. For you, there is great personal satisfaction in seeing how real, living people and organizations benefit. And deeply satisfying personal experiences result from engaging productively with stimulating and interesting people and making new and valuable friendships. Good works do attract good people, and important good works attract the best.

End Notes

1. Richard I. Kirkland Jr., "Should You Leave It All to the Children?" *Fortune*, September 29, 1986.
2. This wisdom comes from Charles W. Collier of Harvard University and his 2006 guidebook, *Wealth in Families*.

CHAPTER 21

THOUGHTS FOR THE WEALTHY

IF YOU ARE SO FORTUNATE AS TO HAVE OVER $20 MILLION, YOU know you have achieved a great success. Congratulations! Only 50,000 Americans have done this well. Hopefully, you also recognize that you have new kinds of problems. If you're uncomfortable or not fully satisfied with mutual funds—though you probably should be satisfied—how do you find investment advisors and investment managers who are right for you? How much do you pass on to your children and grandchildren—how and when? How much do you commit to philanthropy—how and when?

If you have a much larger fortune—over $100 million—you should consider organizing an investment committee or having a personal expert to advise you on all aspects of investing. If paying 2 percent of assets to an investment advisor year after year seems high to you—as it does to me—an alternative is to engage an advisor once every 10 years on a fee-for-time basis to conduct a thorough evaluation of all your financial and investment plans to be sure they make sense for you. (*Tip:* Some of the best informed and most thoughtful investment professionals work at large foundations and educational endowments or at large corporate pension funds and might be glad to help you for a nice per diem compensation—with meetings on weekends.) If your "personal expert" helps save you from one mistake or helps you make one wise move, you'll have found a bargain.

You'll also be wise to retain one of the finest trust and estate lawyers. (*Tip:* Young lawyers can be best because they are still building their practices and will still be practicing many years from now so you and your wealth will have continuing service from the same trusted advisor.) Finally, retain the best young partner in a major accounting firm as an advisor and overseer and jointly hire a superb bookkeeper you personally like to work in your office, keep all the records, report monthly, and "watch the watchmen" by monitoring investments.

If you have substantial wealth, you'll be inundated by delightful, articulate people known in the trade as "asset gatherers" because of their ability to win the trust of wealthy people. You may enjoy seeing how charmingly gifted they can be, but please be cautious and see how sincerely they want you to turn your fortune over to them.

"Alternative" investing has been in the limelight—partly because some practitioners are paid astronomical amounts and make good copy for the media, partly because some have achieved extraordinary investment results, and partly because so many investors hope to find a way to obtain high returns with little risk. In addition, the incentive compensation for their salespeople is truly compelling.

Another reason alternative investing has attracted so much attention is that it has worked well for two of the longest, earliest, and most skillful practitioners: Yale and Harvard. (*Full disclosure:* I served on Yale's investment committee for 16 years.) The results are extraordinary and, equally important, have been achieved systematically and deliberately through a rigorously disciplined process, but they are very hard to replicate.

When friends repeat the line from *When Harry Met Sally*—"I'll have what she's having"—I'm reminded of a growing-up experience. My mother took us to the Ringling Bros. and Barnum & Bailey Circus. Impressed by the daring young acrobats on the flying trapeze, I resolved to try it at home. I got skinned knees, skinned elbows, and a skinned chin—and learned that copying experts is not easy. (Old Wall Street question: "What's the fastest way to make a small future?" Answer: "Start with a large fortune and try to copy the experts.") So here are some friendly warnings about some of the recently popular but unconventional ways to invest.

Hedge funds

Hedge funds have burst onto the scene partly because they performed well in the millennium market collapse of dot-com stocks, but primarily because they offer investment managers an amazingly powerful way to get rich. The 2 percent fee easily covers all costs, plus the manager gets 20 percent of all profits. Learning that smart friends are making $10 million in a single year (or that at least one hedge fund manager made over $1 *billion* in one year) is hard to ignore if you are a gifted investor, young, competitive, and keen to make a fortune yourself and you work in a small shop with several other brilliant people trying to figure things out. It's fun. It's interesting. And when it clicks, you make serious money. Who wouldn't be interested?

Hedge funds come in an infinite variety of strategies, and all are—or certainly seem to be—run by brilliant, intensely striving, extremely confident, fashionably dressed managers with distinguished academic and prior employment records. However, hedge funds basically fall into two very different categories. One kind is managed by supersmart investors—usually trained in arbitrage at a major dealer (often Goldman Sachs)—who love to test their skills against all comers, want the personal and intellectual freedom to run their own small shop, and are remarkably capable of seeing and seizing investment opportunity (and like to get very well paid). The managers of the other kind say all the same things, but their focus is on their payouts, the "2 'n' 20" (2 percent annual fee plus 20 percent of profits) that is the most amazing compensation system ever created.

It's easy to tell which kind is which. The truly stellar hedge funds are all closed to new investors.

Funds of funds may make sense as an "insurance" policy against getting badly screwed, but the cost of that insurance is very high. Chances are that you *will* get an above-average portfolio of hedge funds—but not above average enough to be pleased with the long-term outcome.

The challenge for hedge funds—and for investors investing in hedge funds—is in the numbers. If the rate of return in stocks is 7 percent, the breakeven return for a hedge fund has to be 11.25 percent to cover all the fees. This requires "alpha" (the extra return from superior management) of 4.25 percent—a very large superiority. Some hedge funds will get that high return and some will get more, but that's not the real question. The real question is whether the fund you invest in will do that well year after year—particularly as more money goes into hedge funds that all compete with one another in the search to capture alpha.

Venture capital

Venture capital attracts attention. Over the long term, the surging flow of investment capital going into venture capital funds has been astonishing. No doubt there is romance about discovering explosively successful companies like Apple, Google, eBay, or

Starbucks and making over 100 times your investment. But before considering investing in venture capital, consider the following. Over the past 30 years the median return of the top quartile of venture capital funds was 28 percent—but the median return of *all* venture capital funds was actually less than 5 percent (i.e., less than the returns on Treasury bonds). As Harvard professor Josh Lerner summarizes: "If you're not with the good guys, it's not worth playing." The 10 most successful venture capital organizations made combined profits larger than the total excess returns— returns over and above the S&P 500 index returns—of the entire venture capital industry. In other words, relative to the overall market, all the other funds collectively lost money, gave up liquidity, and took more risk. The leading venture capital firms are continually the leaders—for strong reasons—and the odds are high that they will continue to be the most successful.

The secret to success is no secret. It's not the money. Money to invest is necessary, but it is not nearly sufficient. The best venture capital managers are not simply shrewd backers of exciting new products. They are good at this, of course, but their great strengths are two: They know how to select entrepreneurs, and they know how to help build successful companies. They are certainly not passive investors; they are vigorously active and creative. Savvy budding entrepreneurs learn from already successful entrepreneurs how important the best venture investors can be in helping new companies succeed.

The best venture investors are always in touch with the large, medium, and small companies in their industry. They make sure that the most exciting young stars who might launch new companies know how important their assistance can be—how they make many crucial differences to the fledgling companies they invest in. Specializing in specific aspects of technology, they know all the most effective engineers, salespeople, production managers, and financial people, and they know why these people are effective. They appreciate how particular people can fit together as successful teams. They use this expertise to help their companies get smarter and stronger—and become much more likely to succeed. And they know that effective entrepreneurs almost always change their products and target markets as they learn what works and what doesn't work really well. They don't fixate on products or markets—no matter how exciting—because they know the key to success is always the entrepreneur who has a serious need to succeed.

It's no accident that the winners keep winning. Only one problem: You can't use this insight. Like the best hedge funds, the best venture capital organizations are closed to new investors. In fact, they are already overbooked and unable to accommodate all the money that even their long-standing investor clients want to give them. In addition, some of their previously successful entrepreneurs now have large amounts they'd like to invest, and the venture managers, having made large fortunes in successful past investments, want to invest more of their own fortunes. Long story short: You can't get into the funds you'd want to invest in. The others remind wise investors of Groucho Marx's sardonic remark: "I don't care to belong to any club that will accept me as a member."

Real estate

Real estate has many appeals. A remarkable proportion of the wealthiest individuals and families have made their fortunes in real estate. Tax advantages are a major factor; astute use of leverage and access to credit—lots of it—are important; extraordinary skill at adversarial negotiations is crucial; patience and decisive action are both essential. In addition, success depends on extraordinary, intricate knowledge of all the relevant details of each local market and, within a chosen market, of each property, its tenants and their lease agreements; clever insights into ways specific improvements will significantly enhance future rentals; and a special ability to attract desirable tenants. An absolute devotion to the business is mandatory.

Few people would be willing and able to meet all these requirements, and hardly anybody can hope to succeed on a part-time basis. That's why those who do devote themselves to real estate investing can, if fortune smiles on them, do so very well.

If you want to invest in real estate without making an outsized time commitment, you can invest in REITs (real estate investment trusts) which are listed on the principal exchanges. They trade at prices reflecting both real estate and the overall stock market. Their long-term returns are similar to overall stock returns.

As with other specialized alternative investments, the best *private equity* funds are closed to new investors. That's okay for individual investors because private equity funds—overall and on average—have underperformed the market averages after their substantial leverage is factored in. In other words, investors would be better off—and have more liquidity—by buying publicly traded stocks with moderate margins.

Commodities

Commodities are economically inert and do not develop value, as a result changes in their price are driven by changes in demand or supply. Those who buy and sell commodities are not investing; they are speculating that they know more or better than the market knows. They may be right with their bets and trades, but for every right there must be an equal wrong. The total of all trading adds up to a negative—a zero-sum game minus the costs of trading.

One concluding thought. If you have won the "money game," ask yourself: Is it more important to concentrate on offense to win even more, or is it better to concentrate on defense and lose less?

CHAPTER 22

YOU ARE NOW GOOD TO GO!

YOU—NOT YOUR INVESTMENT MANAGERS—HAVE THE MOST important job in successful investment management. Your central responsibilities are to decide on your long-term investment objectives and determine a reasoned and realistic set of investment policies that can achieve your objectives.

You should study your total investment situation, your emotional tolerance for risk, and the history of investment markets, because a mismatch between the market's sometimes grim realities and your financial and emotional needs can result and has often—and as recently as 2008—resulted in great harm.

Investors who study the realities of investing will be able to protect themselves and their investments from the all too common but unrealistic belief that they can find fund managers who will substantially beat the market. The well-informed investor understands that the only way an active investment manager can beat the market is to find and exploit other investors' mistakes more often than they find and exploit his or her mistakes, and understands that a manager who strives to beat the market is all too likely to try too hard and be beaten instead. Most of the managers and clients who insist on trying—either on their own or with professional managers—will be disappointed by the results. It *is* a loser's game.

Happily, there is an easy way to win the loser's game simply by not playing by the conventional rules that are out of date. Raised in the tradition that says, "If you find a problem, find a solution," I felt intrigued by the task of finding a solution to the problem identified long ago in "The Loser's Game."[1] As is often true, the solution is to "think outside the box" and redefine the problem. Thus, the focus shifted from the loser's game (working ever harder in a futile effort to beat the market) to the winner's game of ignoring Mr. Market and concentrating on the big picture of your longer-term objectives, asset mix, and investment policies—and *staying the course.*

Individual investors are important for three major reasons. First, there are so many—nearly 50 million in the United States and almost as many in other nations. Second, almost all individual investors are truly on their own in designing long-term investment policies and strategies because few investment consultants can afford to provide the counseling most individuals need at a fee they will pay. Third, virtually all how-to books on investing are sold on the false promise that the typical individual can beat the professional investors. He or she can't, and he or she won't.

Fortunately, the individual investor does not have to. Successful investing does not depend on beating the market. Attempting to beat the market—to do better than other investors—will distract you from the fairly simple but interesting and highly productive task of designing a long-term program of investing that will succeed at providing the best feasible results for you.

If you feel, as I do, that some of the advice in this book is pretty simple, remember Warren Buffett's wonderful summary: Investing *is* simple—but it's not easy.[2]

Soundly conceived, persistently followed long-term investment policies are the pathway to success in investing. The actions required are not complicated. The real challenge is to commit to the discipline of long-term investing and avoid the compelling distractions of the excitement that surrounds, but is superfluous to, the real work of investing. This commitment to the discipline of long-term investing is your principal responsibility—and your best opportunity to contribute to your own long-term investing success.

There are two different kinds of problems in trying to beat the market. One problem is that this is extraordinarily difficult to do—and it's all too easy, while trying to do better, to do *worse*. The other problem is that it will divert your attention from the need to establish long-range objectives and investment policies that are well matched to your particular needs.

Winning the loser's game of beating the market is easy: *Don't play it.* Concentrate on the winner's game of defining and adhering faithfully to sound investment policies that are right for the market realities and right for your long-term goals and objectives.

The needs and purposes of different investors are not the same, and their investment portfolios should not be the same. You have already answered the important questions: Where are you and who are you? What are your assets, income, debts, and responsibilities? How do you feel about market risk, and can you trust yourself to be a sensible long-term investor? The answers to these few questions are what make each of us unique as investors.

To fulfill your responsibilities to yourself, you need three characteristics:

1. A genuine interest in developing an understanding of your true interests and objectives.
2. A basic appreciation of the fundamental nature of capital markets and investments, including Mr. Market's clever

tricks and the market dominance of powerful institutional investors.

3. The discipline to work out and hold onto the basic policies that will succeed over time in fulfilling your realistic investment objectives. That's what this book is all about.

While it is a spirited critique of contemporary investment practice, this book is by no means a condemnation of investment managers. The problem is not that professional managers lack skill or diligence. Quite the opposite. The problem with trying to beat the market is that professional investors are so talented, numerous, and dedicated to their work that as a group they make it very difficult for any one of their number—and virtually impossible for individual investors—to do significantly better than others, particularly in the long run. Professional investment managers should encourage their clients to use this book as a guide to performing the vital role of being informed, active, and therefore *successful* clients.

This book is written with a clear point of view: The real purpose of investment management is not to beat the market; it is to do what is right for each particular investor who will accept the central investor responsibility and who wants to be successful at achieving his or her true and realistic objectives. Much as it might seem obvious that investors should care a lot about the way their money is managed, the reality is that they typically do almost nothing about it—until it's too late. This book is written for investors who are prepared to take charge of their own investment destiny.

When you have finished digesting the straightforward propositions presented in this short book, you will know all you will ever need to know to be truly successful with investments. You are now ready to enjoy *winning investing*. You're good to go!

End Notes

1. Written in 1975 for the *Financial Analysts Journal,* where it won the profession's Graham and Dodd Award.
2. Two of my best friends are at the peak of their distinguished careers in medicine and medical research. They agree that the two most important discoveries in medical history are penicillin and washing hands (which stopped the spreading of infection from one mother to another via the midwives who delivered most babies before 1900). What's more, my friends counsel, there's no better advice on how to live longer than to quit smoking and to buckle up when driving. The lesson: Advice doesn't have to be complicated to be good.

CHAPTER 23

PARTING THOUGHTS

OUBT, SAID THE PHYSICIST RICHARD FEYNMAN, IS THE necessary first step toward creativity. So I've learned to double-check my answers, particularly when the evidence seems most confirming, and to ask, "Could I be wrong?" On the main parts of the argument, I'm confident that certain basic structural realities are not going to change:

- The number of brilliant, hardworking investment professionals is not going to decrease enough to convert investing back into the winner's game of the 1950s and 1960s.
- The proportion of transactions controlled by institutions— and the splendid professionals who lead them—will not decline. Investing, therefore, will stay dangerous for even the gifted amateur.
- Maybe some day so many investors will agree to index that the last stock pickers standing will have the field all to themselves. Maybe. But that'll be the day.

Be sure to call me when these things happen. Meanwhile, I've got better things to do—where I can play to win with both my time and my money. And so do you.

SERVING ON AN INVESTMENT COMMITTEE

INSTITUTIONAL INVESTING IS VERY DIFFERENT FROM INDIVIDUAL investing, and that's not just because, to cite Hemingway's classic retort to F. Scott Fitzgerald: "Yes, they have more money." Many of us have the opportunity to serve on the investment committees of endowments, pension funds, or other institutions, and all who serve want to be helpful. Here is a primer on what to expect and how to be helpful.

Most institutional funds are perpetual or nearly perpetual and are governed by committees that delegate investing to external managers. The investment committee's primary responsibility is not investment management, but good governance.

For most investment committees, the main task and responsibility is determining the appropriate long-term investment policies that bring the greatest harmony to the different disciplines of investing and managing the institution's finances. After that comes ensuring that effective working relationships are developed with investment managers. At multibillion-dollar funds, this important work will be done by a full-time staff and overseen by the committee. But for most funds under $1 billion, the manager-selection decisions are the investment committee's responsibility, so committee members will want to be sure they know how to do it right.

As in any good business relationship, the responsibilities and undertakings of each party—the committee, which is the client, and the investment manager—should be realistic and clear to both. In particular, the investment manager's mission should be explicit, in writing, and mutually agreed upon. It should clearly be within the manager's competence and realistic relative to the market, and it should satisfy the committee's informed expectations. If these three criteria are *not* being met, the client should get together with the investment manager for candid discussion until they have agreed on a mission statement that passes all three tests.

The relationship will usually be centered on regular meetings organized to achieve together the success that is desired by both the investment manager and the investment committee. Before each meeting, the committee should establish an agenda, and the investment manager should furnish all relevant documentation for the meeting, allowing ample time for careful preparation by both the manager and the members of the committee.

The emphasis on *relevant* documentation is deliberate. It takes little genius to flood a meeting with enough trivia to obfuscate the central issues.

Every meeting should be designed and controlled by the client—*not* by the manager, as so often happens. It is the client's money, and the purpose of an endowment is to serve the institution's mission.

Investment policy should be separated from investment operations because they are very different responsibilities. All too often, responsibility for investment policy is delegated to fund managers along with the operating management of the portfolio. *Mixing together investment policy and portfolio operations—problem definition and problem solving—and delegating* both *is asking trouble to come find you.* Only by separating portfolio operations from policy formation can responsibility and accountability be established for each of these two different aspects of investment management.

Of course, investment policy and investment operations are not kept in isolation from each other. Operating performance should be evaluated objectively against the specified policy intention to be sure that operations are in accord with policy, and investment policy should be evaluated objectively against long-term returns in the portfolio to be sure that the policies are realistic.

The specialized language derived from modern portfolio theory makes it relatively easy to specify investment objectives and policies. "Sharpe ratios" (a measure of excess returns relative to risk) and "benchmark returns" enable clients to monitor how well portfolio operations conform to agreed-upon policy. This information enables each portfolio manager to achieve good performance—not by heroically "beating the market," but by faithfully and sensibly carrying out realistic investment policies to achieve defined objectives.

The investment committee and its investment managers should agree explicitly on each of these important policy dimensions:

1. The level of market risk to be taken by the portfolio.
2. Whether the level of risk is to be sustained or varied as markets change.
3. Whether individual-stock risk or group (market segment) risk is to be taken or avoided and the incremental rate of return which such risks, when taken, are expected to produce for the portfolio.

Since each investment manager's actual performance will—like the market return—be drawn from a bell-shaped probability distribution around an average rate of return, investment objectives and performance measurements should be specified in terms of both the average rate of return—relative to appropriate benchmarks—and the distribution around that average return. Since a professional investment manager is given more and more discretion to deviate from a market-matching fund and take more and more risks of different kinds—market risk, group risk, and individual-stock risk—the difficulty of determining how much of any specific period's portfolio return is to the result of skill as opposed to chance increases rapidly.

Just as operating performance should be evaluated compared to agreed-upon investment policy, investment policy can be evaluated against long-term operations. If the fund does not achieve the expected investment result, should the policy be changed? Perhaps the objective is too high. Perhaps the guidelines are too restrictive for the objective sought. The asset allocation policy regarding investing in specific classes of stocks—growth stocks, utility stocks, Japanese stocks, whatever—should be evaluated by examining the returns of peer-group portfolios of growth stocks (or utility stocks or Japanese stocks) and in comparison with alternative types of stocks and the market as a whole over relatively long periods. *Note:* Policies are intentionally long term and should be adopted or changed only carefully and slowly. If the policy is found to be inappropriate, however, it should be changed, and the new or modified policy should be explicit—always in writing.

It is by direct comparison with explicit investment policies—and only by comparison with explicit policies—that the operational performance of the investment manager should be measured and evaluated. For example, it would be both unfair and misleading to attempt to evaluate the operational performance of a portfolio of growth stocks by comparing its results with overall market averages. All too often a "growth" specialist or a "small-cap" specialist will be cheered or jeered—equally unfairly—when that type of specialty just happens to be in favor or out of favor in the overall market.

Each meeting with managers should begin with a careful review of the investment manager's agreed-upon mission to see if any modification in objective or policy is appropriate. If neither the client nor the investment manager has any changes in mission to propose, both should explicitly reaffirm the mission statement.

If either the client or the manager wishes to propose a change, the proposal and the rationale supporting it should be prepared in advance and distributed as one of the meeting preparation documents so that all participants can study and think through the proposed change well before coming to the meeting. There should be no surprises in this most important part of the meeting.

Discussion of specific portfolio operations—purchases and sales of specific securities—should be only on an "exception" basis and should be brief. This portion of the meeting should *not* be "interesting." Clients should not accept colorful recitations of war stories or capsule reviews of specific stocks. These *are* fun, but they are only entertainment. Instead, this part of the meeting should be a straightforward confirmation that the manager has sensibly and faithfully followed an agreed-upon policy. Like a successful medical examination, the review of operations should be thorough and expeditious, and it should conclude with the assurance, "As expected, we are achieving your objectives with the concepts and process we promised to use in managing your investments so there's no reason to modify our mandate. We are on target, and everything is fine." Ideally, the review of operations and reaffirmation of the investment manager's mission should take just five minutes. If they take longer, "Houston, we have a problem." Something is wrong: Either the mission is not clear, or the results are off mission.

The balance of the meeting time, usually less than an hour, can best be devoted to a thoughtful and detailed discussion of almost any one or two of the many topics of importance to both the client and the manager as a way of increasing shared understanding of the manager's investing process. Discussion topics could include a major economic development that affects portfolio strategy, or research supporting a major portfolio commitment, or the changing investment attraction of a particular industry. The important purpose of these topical discussions is to enable the committee to take a deep look into the thinking process of the investment manager.

If portfolio operations have not been in accord with agreed-upon policy and the investment manager's agreed-upon mission, it is not really important whether current portfolio results happen to be above (lucky you) or below (unlucky you) the results that would be expected if the policy had been followed faithfully. In either case, the truly important information is that the portfolio and the portfolio manager are out of conformance and inconsistent—and probably out of control. Sooner or later this lack of control will show up in losses—uncontrolled and unrecoverable losses.

The main reason for measuring performance is to improve client-manager communication. The purpose of performance measurement is, not to provide *answers, to identify questions* that investors and managers should explore together to be sure they have a good mutual understanding of what is contributing to and what is detracting from investment performance. Ask the child's favorite series of questions: Why? Why? Why?

Committee members may find that just one or two decisions—perhaps brilliantly skillful, perhaps lucky, perhaps both—can make a powerful difference in the reported performance of a portfolio, particularly in the short term. Professional investment managers will recognize how often one of their portfolios has enjoyed far better results than another portfolio simply because, when implementing a strategic decision to invest heavily in a particular industry group, the specific stock used in one portfolio did very well while the specific stock used in another portfolio did not. The classic example was the impact on American Research

& Development Corporation, a venture capital fund, of a spectacularly successful but small and almost accidentally made investment in Digital Equipment Corporation in 1967. The fund felt it had an obligation to an MIT professor who said he thought he had been promised financial support. With the Digital investment, American Research & Development significantly outperformed the market averages. Without Digital, the fund would have underperformed the market during its 20-year life.

The final area of performance measurement is clearly qualitative. Does the manager's explanation of his or her decisions make good sense? Is the manager doing as promised—making the kinds of decisions that were "advertised"? Are the manager's actions consistent with his or her words at the previous meeting? When the manager changes the portfolio's structure, do the explanations make sense? As a thoughtful, interested client, do you find your confidence in the manager's abilities, knowledge, and judgment rising as you have more and more discussions—or falling? Investors should give real weight to these "soft" qualitative factors because, over and over again, this is where the best signals of real trouble first surface, long before the problem is evident in the hard quantitative data.

At least once a year, there should be a candid review of your institution's overall financial situation—the context in which the investment portfolio fits. Similarly, the investment manager should devote part of one meeting each year to a discussion of his or her organization's professional and business development, with particular emphasis on long-term policies and commitments.

Meetings should *not* be used—as they almost always are—for a brief and ultimately meaningless tour of the investment world that might include superficial comments on the economic outlook, recent changes in interest rates, a review of minor changes in the weightings of industry groups in the equity portfolio, and a quick recap of modest shifts in quality ratings in the bond portfolio, concluding with some "interesting" insights into a few specific decisions.

Like chitchat about individual stocks, such discussions are really just entertainment and can easily deteriorate into a superficial "show and tell" report of current events with each meeting separate from all prior and all future meetings. Without really digging into any of the major decisions made, they can use up time that otherwise might be devoted to serious discussions of subjects of potentially enduring importance to the portfolio and to a successful relationship.

A written summary of perhaps three to five pages should be prepared and distributed after each meeting and kept for future reference. One good suggestion would be to have alternating meetings summarized by the client and the investment manager.

Investment committees have three levels of operational decisions. First, should a manager be changed? The normal expectation is "no." If any manager is identified as up for review, there should be a rigorous analysis of the cases for and against taking action. Give particular care and attention to the case for *not* taking action. Committees all too often drop managers they should keep and switch to managers who have just finished their best periods. The transaction costs of making these changes are high, particularly where the terminated manager goes on to do well and the newly hired manager has already peaked and will underperform after being chosen.

Should the money amounts assigned to specific managers be changed? Experience shows that the best decision is often the counterintuitive one: to assign *more* money to the manager who has been recently *under*performing. Reason: The well-chosen manager will probably be underperforming only because his or her style is temporarily out of favor in the market and probably will outperform when market conditions are more favorable to his or her style.

Should the long-term policy on asset mix be changed? If not, would a significant temporary deviation be appropriate? If not, the work of the client is over—and the formal part of the meeting over, too.

In this format, decisions are on an exception basis. Decisions to act are few and far between because you will have already done the homework rigorously, will know your true objectives, and will have decided on sensible long-term investment policy *and* on the specific mission for each manager. Having made decisions for the long term, you should need to make few, if any, changes.

How long should an ideal meeting take? Actually, about five minutes—with no actions taken because none are needed. As every experienced manager of continuous-process factories knows, one indication of a well-run continuous process, such as investment management, is that nothing interesting is going on because anything interesting is a problem. A well-run continuous-processing plant is problem-free and does not need corrections.

The most important contribution an investment committee can make to a successful relationship with an investment manager is to select the *right* manager to begin with. A prospective investment management firm should have a clear concept of how it will add value in managing client portfolios. That concept can be based on the manager's perception of a kind of *opportunity* or a kind of *problem* that presents favorable chances for this particular firm to increase the portfolio's rate of return. In addition to a cogent concept of how to add value, the investment manager should have developed a clear, sensible process for making decisions to implement that concept and should have a valid record of achievement.

Here are some of the questions investment committees might ask prospective investment managers and pursue to full understanding:

- How have your investment management concepts and process changed in the past decade? Why? How might they change in the *next* decade?
- What does your firm do because you believe it's right even though it costs you money? And what do you *not* do even though it would be profitable?
- How have you changed your business strategy in the past? How might you change it in the future? Why?
- What is the compensation of your senior people and how is it determined?
- What investment results have you achieved for *each* of your 25 largest clients—and how do you explain any differences?

Keep notes on the answers your investment manager gives to your questions for future use in comparing the answers you get at other times to the same or similar questions. (This simple technique has been used for years—perhaps even for centuries—by the managers of the Scottish investment trusts and by the Japanese because it works so well.) If and when you decide to terminate an investment manager, do yourself a favor and recognize that the failure may not be the manager's; it may be yours. So don't go looking for a new manager until you've taken the time and care to learn how you could do a better job of selecting and working with each of your managers. Chances are that you did not define with rigor the mission for which the manager was hired, you were not as diligent as you should have been in determining the manager's ability to complete the mission successfully, or you did not communicate to the manager all you could have about your aspirations and expectations.

The concept of using multiple managers has become increasingly popular among large funds in recent years. Several reasons are given:

- You can select specialist managers skilled in each of the different kinds of investing wanted.
- Clients can diversify to protect themselves against the risk of any one manager's investment concept being out of tune with the overall market (as will surely happen from time to time).
- Managers who fail to perform can be terminated more easily when they manage only part of your funds.
- Maybe most important, investment consultants—paid for conducting manager searches—much prefer to see multiple managers. The more, the merrier. With 15 to 30 different managers, there's always one manager "in the penalty box." Glad to oblige, the consultant agrees to do another search, collect a fee, and keep the ball rolling.

The problem with multiple managers is that the first three positive reasons above become decreasingly powerful as the number of managers increases. While it may be feasible to select one or two superior managers in a particular specialty, it's harder to pick several. There just aren't that many truly superior managers around. And wise selections take time.

Although diversification does increase with each additional manager, when the separate funds are amalgamated into one and analyzed, it becomes clear that each additional fund adds less and less incremental diversification but does incur higher and higher operating costs and fees—and moves the whole portfolio closer and closer to the investment characteristics of an index fund.

Since index funds are readily available at low cost, the use of different managers cannot be justified as a way to diversify and reduce risk. That can be accomplished much more easily and cheaply with a simple, broad market index fund.

If a client is prepared to pay the higher fees inherent in having multiple managers, the objective must be to increase returns by finding specialist managers who can identify and will exploit the occasional opportunities that may arise from the mispricing errors of other managers. Realistically, important opportunities of this kind are rare. So a fund with multiple managers will almost certainly be overpaying for excess diversification.

The argument that managers can be more easily terminated— with less harm to the fund and less harm to the management firm—if the account is relatively small for both parties is, of course, true, but it may be pernicious. Committees may be less careful in selecting or supervising managers they know they can readily terminate.

Endowment funds under $5 billion should especially consider rejecting the strategy of deploying assets in specialist assignments to numerous active managers. A few of the leading passive (index fund) management companies and some of the leading active managers are now offering a wide array of investment capabilities and a client-centered portfolio consulting service that customizes portfolios to each client's objectives and adapts each portfolio to changing market conditions.

Thoughtful observers are increasingly in agreement that investment committees have important governance responsibilities to ensure the successful management of the endowments that support many of our nation's most treasured institutions. While the full board of trustees has the ultimate institutional responsibilities, the center of good governance for endowments is the investment committee.

If you serve on the investment committee of an endowment (or pension fund), you may be in for an early surprise. While some institutional investors have well-reasoned and well-developed investment programs, all too many do not. Sadly, their investment managers and consultants are not doing much to help. They too are improvising in ever-changing markets—with the best intentions, of course. Committee members can learn useful lessons from the best-practices investment committees.

In multibillion-dollar endowments, good *governance* is not operational *management* such as selecting and working with individual managers. Committees that focus on good governance will be fully occupied with such responsibilities as:

- Approving portfolio structure
- Overseeing the process of investment manager selection
- Recommending the appropriate spending rule—the percentage of total assets that the institution can spend each year—to the full board of trustees
- Ensuring ample capacity and skill within the investment office
- Serving as a board of review on compensation, recruiting, and staff development
- Ensuring that the endowment is optimally integrated with the institution

Best-practices investment committees focus on achieving sustainable long-term positive investment results through wise policies, appropriate long-term goals and objectives, and careful selection of operating managers. That's what endowments and their investment committees are really for and that's why donors entrust their funds to them.

Who should serve on a best-practices investment committee? In investing, experience is not only the best teacher; it's the only good teacher. Investment committees need thoughtful and informed members ready and able to make judgments based on the kind of wisdom that can only come from experience in investing, so a majority of the members of each investment committee should have substantial experience as investors. A minority of committee members may be chosen for other reasons: experience as business leaders, expertise and understanding of the institution and its finances, or demonstrated philanthropic generosity. All members should have demonstrated good judgment of people, concepts, and organizations.

The organization's president should always serve on or meet regularly with the investment committee to ensure understanding by the committee of the institution's financial management challenges—near and long term—and appreciation of the long-term program strategy and plans for fund-raising. And, vice versa, institutional and financial managers setting the plans and budgets and leading the fund-raising for the institution need to understand the realities of endowment management. As in any really good relationship, success depends on good communication both ways.

Service on committees should be staggered and planned. Terms of five or six years—renewable once or even twice—help committees remove quietly those who are ineffective or not enjoying service. Members should differ in background, age, and skills, but should all be proficient on one criterion: "plays well with others." Tenure on best-practices committees should *average* six to eight years; for all sorts of working groups, this proves to be optimal. Shorter average tenure often means that members are too new to each other to know how to be great "co-listeners" and how to work as a true team. Longer average tenure can mean that members have stopped listening carefully to one another.

By clearly separating the work of management from the work of governance, best-practices investment committees demonstrate that they understand that good governance provides the long-term policy framework and ensures the working environment that enables operating managers to do their work both efficiently and effectively.

The best investment committees make sure that investment managers are skillful, diligent, and cost-effective in investment *operations,* but their primary focus and responsibility is on getting it really right on governance and investment *policy.* Every endowed institution is unique, and each deserves its own custom-tailored set of governance policies on risk, strategic portfolio structure, and spending.

Investment committees—usually meeting four times each year—have two reasons for concentrating on governance and not attempting management. First, in today's intensely managed, fast-changing capital markets, committees meeting quarterly are ill-suited for taking up operational decisions. They can't do it well. Second, even the best-organized and best-led committees will find themselves fully challenged by the responsibilities of good governance: setting appropriate limits on risk, setting optimal investment policies and objectives, agreeing on portfolio structure, ensuring wise selection of investment managers, staying on a steady course during periods of market euphoria and market anxieties and fears, formulating sensible spending rules, and coordinating with the finance committee and the full board of trustees so that endowment investment management performs its full and appropriate role in the overall fiscal governance of the institution. Wise integration of endowment investing, institutional finance, and fund-raising is, of course, the central responsibility of the board of trustees, but this important "macro" strategy work can often be best initiated and even led by the investment committee.

While all investment committees are, of course, interested in good long-term rates of return, the best practitioners know that their first priority must always be managing risks, particularly in buoyant times when risks are easily overlooked. In particular, market risks can be translated through an appropriate spending rule into smoothed and predictable flows thus avoiding disruptive risks to the institution's ability to consistently support its mission or interfering with fund-raising by upsetting donors.

Risk management most definitely does not mean overly conservative "caution." As Robert Barker's committee reported to the Ford Foundation, the opportunity cost of excessive caution can be immense when it constricts an institution from achieving its public purpose. The sad history of failures and shortfalls in institutional investing has more examples of too little than of too much courage in investing. Best-practices investment committees will insist on taking and managing sensible short-term risks, seen as daily, weekly, and yearly market fluctuations, and insist on avoiding unnecessary long-term risks of real loss—through either overreaching or not striving. Each can bring permanent loss.

As children, we were raised on the Biblical parable of the three servants and their talents —a talent was a monetary unit as well as a skill. It taught that the son who kept but did not invest or use his talents was a woeful failure nearly as contemptible as the profligate son who spent all of his on entertainments. By no means should risk management guidelines provide a hiding place for investment policies or practices that are unwisely overconservative. Astute risk management both avoids insufficiently rewarded risk (speculation) and abhors excessive caution. Best-practices investment committees make certain that they secure the defensive perimeter with "active reconnaissance"—with specific members being responsible for keeping well informed about each investment manager's organization, its professional capacities, and its business commitments and for being actively engaging in "scuttlebutt" networks and regularly revisiting each manager at his or her office to watch for changes that might be early warning signals. Best-practices investment committees search continuously and diligently for the right balance between risk and reward. For them, boldly cautious is no oxymoron.

Good governance will avoid "trying too hard" to increase returns; will ensure that only "all-weather" managers with strong professional organizational cultures are selected; and will set spending rules that can and will be sustained indefinitely "for richer, for poorer; in sickness, and in health." Achieving strong rates of return will require being bold, but not too bold, and modern, but not too modern. Investment professionals learn slowly and only through painful experience not to follow the crowd, particularly when a crowd is enamored of the view through the rearview window of recent experience and the recent past is projected as easy glories to come for those who join the parade late in the day.

The central governance decision will be deciding the degree of emphasis on equity investment. For long-term returns, the equity emphasis should be substantial. Where should investment committees turn for advice? First, every committee member should read the most thoughtful and useful book ever written on endowment investing, *Pioneering Portfolio Management* by David Swensen[1], who, for over a quarter century, has been taking good risks, avoiding bad risks, and building an outstanding record of boldly conservative investing for Yale University. Swensen's thoughtful and explicit explanation of the reasoning behind each aspect of Yale's endowment clearly invites—even obliges—every other institution to develop its own answers to each of the core questions:

- What is your strategic portfolio structure and *why?*
- How do you select investment managers and *why?*
- What is your spending rule and *why?*
- What are your investment committee's particular functions and responsibilities and *why?*

Good governance centers on ensuring that investment operations are within the skills of the particular institution. The easiest operation uses index funds. If active management is considered, best-practices committees will start with a rigorous review of long-term results—at *least* 10 years—which will show clearly that most managers fail to match, let alone beat, the index (and that the average shortfall is larger than the average value added). Committees should also examine objectively the probability that they will be able to select the manager who will outperform in the future. Many have tried this, and most have *not* succeeded.

If active managers are to be used, most small and midsized endowments should consider using one manager with many different demonstrated skills managing a full spectrum of different kinds of stocks and bonds. By concentrating all the assets with one multicapability firm, even a small endowment makes itself a major account—which will justify the manager giving it "blue ribbon" attention. Having too many managers is costly. The obvious cost is that when your total fund is divided into many small accounts, your fund gets charged the high end of the managers' fee structures. Other costs are hidden, but they can be far more consequential.

Wise spending and wise investing are the two hands clapping in support of well-governed, well-managed institutions. *Note:* spending should conform to and be determined by investment results, not the other way around. Trustees should never let spending wishes or "needs" influence—let alone determine— investment objectives or investment management. Making sure of this fiscal discipline is clearly the responsibility of the investment committee.

Compensation and incentives for the investment staff should be aligned with the endowment's objectives. Since investing has a long wavelength, compensation should be based on a three- to five-year moving average with annual written evaluations of achievements relative to explicit and agreed-upon priorities.

Investment committees can make a major contribution to good governance by establishing clear policies on the selection of managers. For an endowment large enough to support an operating staff, this does not mean that the committee will actually select— or terminate—managers. In fact, the best evidence of a committee that is confused about the separation of governance versus management is that the committee hires and fires managers. Committees are notoriously not good at making tough calls in a timely manner. But committees can and should require explicit statements of the policies and practices that will be used in selecting or terminating investment managers:

- How many managers will be used—and why?
- What will be the maximum and minimum size of each manager's mandate—and why?
- What selection criteria and "due diligence" process will be followed—and why?
- What criteria will be used for manager terminations—and why?

The expected duration of each manager relationship is very long—ideally *forever*. Forever may seem an unrealistically long time. It's not. The cost of changing managers for high turnover funds can be far greater than the 3 to 5 percent transaction costs usually cited; the all-in cost includes the cost of hiring "hot" managers *high* and firing disappointing managers *low* and selecting managers almost casually, knowing they may only be temporary so real rigor is not fully recognized as essential. Quickly chosen managers will disappoint all too soon. And changing managers can become a costly habit.

Add to these costs the hidden costs of distracting the committee and management from working more rigorously on their real responsibility of developing superb working relationships with their best managers. While committees all blame the turnover on the managers, the real culprits are the committees. They hire impatiently—often on only a one-hour "speed dating" presentation. Then, because the main consideration is "good performance" versus the market rather than a well-developed shared understanding between the investment committee and each manager, they repeat the in-and-out, in-and-out sequence—increasing the frustrations of both managers and committees. Both know there must be a better way.

Investment committees that want to be best practitioners will benefit from careful self-study to see if any of these signs of trouble are part of their problem:

- *Overdiversification and having too many managers.*

  Having many managers may be a necessity for the largest endowments when they also decide to use small specialist managers. Rarely is a manager skilled at both investing in conventional asset classes and in "alternatives" such as private equity, real estate, and hedge funds, so committees that want both types of investing will usually need both types of managers.

  While there are potential benefits to diversifying managers and having experts in each asset class or specialty, history teaches us that the benefits of diversification among managers with the same basic mandate are, particularly in the long run, modest. After all, most managers already diversify portfolios across 80 to 100 different stocks. With numerous managers, the committee will never develop with any of its managers the shared understanding that is needed to develop superb trust-based, open relationships that enable client and manager to work well together to add value.

  With a dozen or more managers, at least one will invariably be "on watch" or "in the penalty box," so the

committee's limited time will get focused on solving
problems rather than adding value. Not really knowing each
manager well enough to weather stormy passages,
committees will be tempted to bury mistakes and "throw the
bums out," incurring the 3 to 5 percent cost of changing
managers and repeating the sad cycle again and again.

- *Rotating committee members too quickly.*

Some regular turnover is good and helps keep the
committee and its discussions fresh, but if members come on
and go off too quickly, they will miss the privilege of
learning how best to work together and the group will lose
the stabilizing benefits of institutional memory. Committee
members should also not stay too long. They'll get stale and
will stop listening closely to each other. Some will even
begin acting as proprietors, which is wrong; they are
supposed to be serving as fiduciaries, not owners.

- *Allowing one or two committee members to dominate.*

The chairs of best-practices investment committees are
servant-leaders who take as their top priority facilitating the
collective contributions of *all* committee members. This
facilitation begins with selecting members who play well
with others *and* have expertise to contribute. It extends
through thoughtful preparation of the agenda and
documentation so that important policy issues are given
ample time for full discussion *and* resolution. And it includes
attending to the climate of meetings so they are interesting,
enjoyable, give everyone the chance to be heard, and operate
at "due deliberate speed."

- *Overreliance on investment consultants.*

Make no mistake, no matter how much an investment
consultant exudes the trappings of professionalism,
investment consulting is a business—particularly for the
larger consulting organizations that flourish in the breeding

ground of uncertain, insecure committees looking to rely on data-resplendent "experts" for policy guidance. One big investment consultant, the Frank Russell Company, was sold in 1998 for $1 billion; the head of another consulting firm owns more than one private jet.

The business strategy of investment consulting firms usually involves guiding clients into extensive asset-class diversification which leads directly to having so many investment managers—none of which is really known to the committee—that the committee becomes dependent on the consultant for monitoring and managing the managers. As a result, available time at meetings gets taken up with the interesting and entertaining but eventually fruitless business of firing the "poor performers" and hiring promising "winners" in a repetitive cycle that could only please a Las Vegas marriage parlor.

- *Excessive turnover of investment managers.*

The best practitioners have an *average* tenure or duration of manager relationships of more than 10 years. While an average relationship duration of less than 10 years can be acceptable, an average of only 5 years is not. The best practitioners will focus on selecting and working with management organizations so well that their average tenure will be more than 15 years.

One exception to staying the course with managers is clear: When one of your managers brings the "good" news that he or she has joined forces with—code for sold out to—a major organization (usually a giant bank or insurance company, often domiciled in a different country) that will somehow provide all the resources needed to do great things, do not wait or seek to understand. Terminate immediately. If this view seems too categorical, offer to stay in touch during the next one or two years and, if you are thrilled by the results of the combination—sure to be a great rarity—consider rehiring the terminated manager. But when first told, do not compromise or hesitate.

You will surely receive a brilliantly articulate and often quite moving explication. Personal charm and warm promises will be provided in generous supply, but the long history of such acquisitions is not at all encouraging. So be guided by history and terminate promptly.

A second exception requires particular vigilance: When a manager changes its tune—moving away from the investment philosophy and decision-making process by which it earned the mandate to manage part of your endowment—or when it outgrows the asset size it had declared was its "sweet spot" and maximum aspiration, beware! Experience says that that manager has probably shifted his or her real focus from professional investing to the "asset gathering" business. Such a shift can be remarkably profitable for the managers, but all too costly for the clients.

- *Not measuring results by asset class versus peers.*

   Managers, custodians, or investment consultants can provide the relevant comparative data for each asset class as part of their standard service. Best-practices committees know to read and interpret performance data over time and in the context of reasonable expectations. And they use annual and quarterly comparisons for only one purpose: to encourage the managers to explain the real reasons for results that differ modestly from expectation. Of course, any major difference from expectation may signal a major problem. If so, best-practices committees will address it rigorously.

- *Staff turnover.*

   Endowment management is different from mere portfolio management. It is a calling and a way of making a life, not just a living, and it depends on a strong understanding of the often subtle realities of the particular institution and its leadership. This takes care and time—and they both require continuity. Long-serving capable staff can make important contributions to good governance, so best-practices committees make sure they have able, committed staff members and make sure the staff members are "career." Usually fewer and better can be combined.

- *Selecting top-quartile managers as a policy.*

    Of course, if you always had top-quartile managers, your investment experience would be highly favorable, but the recorded data are overwhelming. Almost nobody has done it for long. Those who harbor such hopes are deluding themselves and sooner or later damage their funds. The irony is that pressing to have the "best" managers all too often leads to hiring hot managers at the peak of their performance records and actively getting subpar results as peaks lead to troughs.

- *Not investing internationally.*

    Diversification *is* the one "free lunch" for investors, and diversification across economies makes sense. However, most funds in most countries are concentrated in their home market.

- *Not considering indexing.*

    The obvious advantage of indexing is lower costs, but that's not as important over the long run as the better investment results. And that's not nearly as important as this: Indexing keeps the committee focused on what really matters—getting it right on the asset mix.

- *Policies not clear and in writing.*

    The ideal set of investment policies could be given to a group of "competent strangers" with confidence that they could follow the stated policies faithfully and return the portfolio in good condition 10 years later.

Assuming the self-evaluation is positive, best-practices committees will focus on policies. The spending rule is the principal connection between the endowment and the budget of the institution. While a variety of choices continues to be used at different institutions, best-practices increasingly centers on the work of Yale's Nobel economist James Tobin, who formulated a sophisticated process to achieve what he wisely called "intergenerational equity." Tobin described this objective eloquently:

> *The trustees of an endowed institution are the guardians of the future against the claims of the present. Their task is to preserve equity among generations. The trustees of an endowed university [or other major institution] . . . assume the institution to be immortal. They want to know, therefore, the rate of consumption from endowment that can be sustained indefinitely. . . . In formal terms, the trustees are supposed to have a zero rate of time preference.*
>
> *Consuming endowment income so defined means in principle that the existing endowment can continue to support the same set of activities that it is now supporting.*

Deciding how much to draw from an endowment for current expenses and how much to continue investing for the future and future spending is one of the most important responsibilities of any investment committee. Some commonly used approaches include the following:

- *All cash income—and no more—is spent.* This is the traditional division between capital and income commonly used in personal trusts. However, with lower rates of dividend payout on common stocks and the recognition that part of any interest payment is really just an offset to inflation and not true income, most institutions do not see this rule as realistic or fair and prefer to pay out a judicious amount that can be sustained over the long term. Most institutions' payouts cluster around 4.5 to 5 percent of assets. Some, unfortunately, concentrate their portfolios in high-yield investments, a practice that typically leads to low-growth equity investments and excessively high bond ratios, which conspire, in different ways, to impoverish the future returns.

A set rate of annual spending means that spendable income to the institution will fluctuate with the market. The sharp global equity market decline during the liquidity crisis of 2008 provided a dramatic example of how much markets— and fixed or semifixed percentage spending—can fall.

- *A set rate can be based on a three-year—or longer—moving average of endowment value.* Tobin takes this idea to a higher level. In Tobin's formulation, designed to achieve intergenerational equity and reasonable stability, actual spending rises and falls with the market—but gradually. Seventy percent of this year's draw is equal to 70 percent of last year's draw (inflated by HEPI: higher education price inflation), and 30 percent varies according to the institution's long-term policy on the rate of spending—usually 4.5 to 5 percent of current endowment value.[2]

Whatever spending rule is adopted, two cardinal principles should govern: *The rule should be set at a level that will be sustained through major bull and bear markets, and the difference between rate of return and spending—that is, the amount that gets reinvested in the endowment—should be enough to absorb fully the corrosive powers of inflation.*

Trustees should be wary of three temptations. One is to believe that the institution's current budgetary priorities are so brilliantly conceived and so vital to the institution's mission that it's okay "on this watch" to make an exception and increase spending above the spending rule. Another is to become so optimistic after a long, favorable market with high returns that the committee says, "This time it's different," and ramps up spending to what may soon prove to be an unsustainably high level that would be painful to bring down.

The third temptation is to decide during a long bear market that the needs of the present are so desperate that heavy drains on the endowment—caused by selling low in a seriously adverse market—are an institutional imperative. *Note:* the best time to prevent this problem is to retard spending increases when markets are *favorable* and the idea of increasing the institution's program budget is most tempting. Markets fluctuate, and so do endowments. Spending rules really matter most when they are accepted as binding even when that discipline is most difficult to accept.

Many investment committees are being advised by consultants to adopt the Harvard-Yale model and make major commitments to "alternative" investments in hedge funds of various types, styles, and kinds, such as private equity, real estate, and venture capital. The past record achieved at Harvard and Yale seems compelling, but wise trustees will be alert to four different factors:

- Strong past returns have attracted huge new inflows, creating what practitioners, echoing Hawaiian surfboarders, call a "wall of money." While the supply of great ideas may increase some, the inevitable reality is that overall returns have and will be substantially reduced as increases in assets outpace returns.
- Demand creates supply. Recognizing the large profits to managers, new firms continue to be formed to capitalize on

any major new opportunity. Some will prove to be great firms and will deliver good returns. But some will prove to be selfish predators feeding on hopeful investment committees. As supply responds to demand and new firms come into the field, the probabilities are great of a decline in professional skill and commitment accompanying a rise in business profit motivation. Caveat emptor—particularly those coming late to the party.

- Consultants overemphasize their roles at the leading universities that they were early investors in alternative asset classes. While consultants were "present at the creation" and provided comparative data and historical market information and sometimes acted as facilitators, they were not concept originators. It's at least possible that their enthusiasm for replication is influenced—if not driven—by their firms' own economic interest in gaining subtle control over committees. They may do this by making the process of supervising numerous different kinds of managers so complex that committees will cede control of quarterly meetings—and thus control over the overall process—to the consultants. Committee members come and go, but the shrewd consultants make themselves a "permanent party." Firms compensate their individual consultants for not losing their clients and keep raising the fees as more and more managers and more and more services are used. Once the substantial base costs of research are covered, the incremental costs to deliver to additional clients are small, so the incremental profits can be truly compelling. You get the picture.

- Many large, medium, and small endowments' investment committees have been vigorously encouraged—some might say near stampeded—into following a remarkably successful way of investing called by a blandly benign designation, the "endowment model." One of my great privileges in a very fortunate life has been to serve for many years on Yale's investment committee and to enjoy a front-row seat watching David Swensen and his team bring the endowment model to vibrant life, producing a truly marvelous record of strong rates of return.

It would be a shame if Swensen's great work was misunderstood or, worse, misinterpreted and converted into a simplistic "anyone can do it" proposition that could lead some investment committees into unwise practices. As in any skill-based line of work, good concepts are necessary, but success is 99 percent skill, experience, and disciplined *execution*. The leading universities have strong, tough-minded, and hardworking teams focused on finding and working with the very best managers—often at very early stages. And they are deep into the scuttlebutt network, exchanging leads, views, and information with other leaders. Reproducing all these advantages is very difficult.

Best-practices committees evaluate their own members and their operation as a committee. What are we doing right? Where can we improve? What should we add to our agenda? Where can we cut? Some best-practices committees also evaluate each member, usually annually, using scale ratings on half a dozen agreed-upon key criteria:

- Comes well prepared
- Stays focused on topic
- Adds value on substance
- Adds value on process
- Inspires confidence in judgment
- Speaks briefly and to the point

The chair reports individual results to each member, with a comparison to the group's high, median, and low scores.

In 2008, investors saw the worst market disruption in a very long time. Two obvious questions came to everyone's mind. First, what should be done? Second, what enduring lessons could be drawn from that dreadful experience?

The realistic and sensible answers to the first question come in two parts. First, if any inappropriate risks were taken, stop doing that. Bank balances over the FDIC-insured maximum are a familiar illustration; those balances should be divided among more banks. Securities should not be left in street name with stockbrokerage firms. Investment managers should be expected to be sure that they too are taking prudently defensive postures.

The second part of the answer to the first question is for most investment committees both more useful and more important. Black swans—unexpected events—do exist. And bell-shaped probability curves do have "fat tails," meaning that the least probable events occur more frequently and with greater impact than a perfectly normal distribution of probabilities would indicate.

Wise investment committee members will not go too close to the edge. After all, Long Term Capital Management's computer models did prove to be right—in the long run—but the giant hedge fund went bankrupt anyway. (Readers may recall the sad report of the driver who knew he had the right of way as he sped through the intersection: He was right, dead right, but he's dead anyway.)

Investment committees pondering the lessons of the cataclysmic events of 2008 will be wise to take another lesson from wise old Ben Graham and never invest in anything without having an adequate "margin of safety" or capacity to absorb error. If precise calculation is required, do not go there.

A final word: Serving on an endowment investment committee should be interesting, enjoyable, and fulfilling. If your committee does not measure up on all three criteria, change it. If you really can't change it, resign—and serve elsewhere. Best-practices committees are designed to be successful on all three dimensions. There's no reason not to be on a best-practices investment committee. Sure, it takes thoughtful determination and leadership, but it's also more fun.

End Notes

1. Swensen, David, *Pioneering Portfolio Management* (New York/London: Free Press, 2003)
2. At Yale, thanks to favorable investment results, funds coming from the endowment had risen from 10 percent of the university budget to over 40 percent. So the trustees, led by the investment committee, shifted the 70:30 ratio to 80:20 to ensure more year-to-year consistency in the flows into the university's budget. Also, as the structure of the Yale endowment's investment portfolio gained more and more stability through diversification by investing more of the total portfolio for absolute than for relative rates of return, the payout ratio was increased, in four stages, from 4.25 percent to 5.25 percent

RECOMMENDED READING

IF YOU WISH TO READ MORE, AS I HOPE YOU WILL, HERE ARE 10 choices you'll find both enjoyable and very worthwhile.

1. *Berkshire Hathaway Annual Reports*. Warren Buffett, widely recognized as our most successful investor, explains with some humor and much candor what he and his partner Charlie Munger are doing and why. Delightful as recreational reading and profoundly instructive, these remarkable annual reports are an open classroom for all investors. The justly famous annual meetings of Berkshire's stockholders are equally candid, entertaining, and informative. Current and past years' reports are available at berkshirehathaway.com.

2. *The Intelligent Investor* by Benjamin Graham, the acknowledged founder of the profession of investment management. This is an "advanced primer." Jason Zweig, deservedly one of the most popular commentators on investing, has published a shrewdly annotated edition (Harper Business Essentials) full of contemporary insights and perspective. If you want more depth, breadth, and

rigor, turn to *Security Analysis* (McGraw-Hill), which is often called Graham and Dodd after its authors. For 70 years, through six editions, it has been the professional investor's bible.

3. *John Bogle on Investing: The First 50 Years* (McGraw-Hill). Jack Bogle is the tribune for the individual investor, the founder of Vanguard, and a crusader with the odd but delightful quirk of thinking clearly, writing well, and having a lot to say that we can all treasure and use.

4. *Pioneering Portfolio Management* (Free Press). David Swensen, Yale's remarkably successful chief investment officer, explains how to manage a large tax-exempt portfolio in a thoroughly modern way with no jargon, no complex equations, and lots of good thinking and judgment. Fully accessible to serious amateurs, this is the best book ever written about professional investing.

5. *Why Smart People Make Big Money Mistakes—and How to Correct Them* by Gary Belsky and Thomas Gilovich (Simon & Schuster). This is an engaging, easy read about how and why we blunder with money decisions and how to defend ourselves against ourselves and our all too human proclivities.

6. *The Crowd* by Gustave Le Bon (Dover Publications). This book, first published long ago, shows that intelligent people lose their rationality and individuality when they join groups or, worse, become part of a crowd. Investors exhibit "crowd behavior" all too often, creating bubbles and panics.

7. *The Only Investment Guide You'll Ever Need* by Andrew Tobias (Mariner Books) is an easy-reading primer without any patronizing. It is clear, comprehensive, candid, and charming. No wonder it has sold over one million copies.

8. *A Random Walk Down Wall Street* by Burton Malkiel (W. W. Norton). Having also sold over a million copies,

this popular and engaging guide to what the professionals know—and all investors should know—provides straight talk from one of Princeton's favorite professors.

9. *An Investor's Anthology* (John Wiley & Sons) is a collection of justly famous insights and ideas that "ring the bell" for professional investors. Seminal papers of great influence that are abstruse or opaque were deliberately excluded.

10. *Wealthy and Wise* (Little, Brown) is Claude N. Rosenberg's thoughtfully challenging explanation of how to recognize how much of your wealth and income you could reinvest in philanthropy and thereby enrich your life.

Some of the best writing and thinking about investing comes from four journalists. I try to take in everything they have to say: Carol Loomis of *Fortune*, Floyd Norris of *The New York Times*, Jason Zweig of *The Wall Street Journal*, and on TV, Consuelo Mack.

INDEX

ABOUT THE AUTHOR

Charles D. Ellis founded and served for 28 years as managing partner of Greenwich Associates, the global leader in strategy consulting to professional financial service firms, and consulted with the world's leading investment managers and securities firms in the United States, Australia, New Zealand, Canada, Japan, Germany, and the United Kingdom. His path-breaking paper "The Loser's Game," published in the *Financial Analysts Journal*, won the profession's Graham and Dodd Award for excellence in 1975.

The author of 15 books and over 100 articles on investing and finance, Ellis has taught the advanced investment courses at Harvard Business School and the Yale School of Management. In addition to chairing CFA Institute, the investment management profession's worldwide association, and being one of only a dozen leaders honored by the Institute for lifetime contributions to the investment profession, he has served as a trustee of Phillips Exeter Academy, an overseer of the Stern Schools of Business at New York University, a trustee of the Robert Wood Johnson Foundation, chairman of the Whitehead Institute for Biomedical Research, successor trustee and for many years chair of the investment committee of Yale University, and as a director of Vanguard.

In recent years, Ellis has served as an advisor to large institutional funds and investors in Australia, New Zealand, Singapore, Vietnam, Saudi Arabia, the United Kingdom, and the United States. His most recent book, *The Partnership*, published by Penguin Press, is a critical examination of the remarkable rise of Goldman Sachs.